A Singularly Unfeminine Profession

One Woman's Journey in Physics

Mary K Gaillard

UC Berkeley

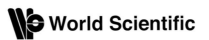

World Scientific

NEW JERSEY · LONDON · SINGAPORE · BEIJING · SHANGHAI · HONG KONG · TAIPEI · CHENNAI

Published by

World Scientific Publishing Co. Pte. Ltd.

5 Toh Tuck Link, Singapore 596224

USA office: 27 Warren Street, Suite 401-402, Hackensack, NJ 07601

UK office: 57 Shelton Street, Covent Garden, London WC2H 9HE

British Library Cataloguing-in-Publication Data
A catalogue record for this book is available from the British Library.

A SINGULARLY UNFEMININE PROFESSION
One Woman's Journey in Physics

ISBN 978-981-4644-22-8
ISBN 978-981-4713-22-1 (pbk)

In-house Editor: Song Yu

Typeset by Stallion Press
Email: enquiries@stallionpress.com

Printed in Singapore

A Singularly Unfeminine Profession:

One Woman's Journey in Physics

Mary K. Gaillard

Dedicated to

Malcolm, Cleo, Julien, Milo, Matisse, Kaeli and Jackendy
and in memory of Bruno Zumino, April 28, 1923–June 21, 2014

Preface

A couple of years after I retired from teaching, I was contacted by an old friend and colleague, Gino Segrè, and I arranged for him to give a talk at Lawrence Berkeley National Laboratory (LBNL). The talk, entitled "The Story of Two Physicists who Changed Science," was based on his book of the same title, his third on the history of science. We had become friends in the early 1960s when Gino was a postdoctoral fellow at CERN, a particle physics laboratory in Geneva, Switzerland. After his talk at Berkeley we had a very enjoyable dinner with my husband, Bruno Zumino, Gino, his wife Bettina, my LBNL colleague Bob Cahn and his wife Fran. After Bob and Fran had left, and we were all about to leave, Bettina looked at me and said: "When are you going to write your book?" In response to my startled reaction she said something to the effect that I had a responsibility to encourage young women who were aspiring scientists. So I started mulling over the idea.

A few days later I had lunch with a group of women graduate students, as the first in a series of meetings they were planning to organize with women faculty. We started chatting about issues of sexual harassment that had been the subject of recent meetings in the department. Then one of them said: "Tell us about your own experiences." I realized that was what they were really interested in. After I recounted some of my worst experiences, especially during my first year as a graduate student in Paris, I was asked why I hadn't given up. I answered in part that I had once been told by Leon Lederman, my friend of many years, that I had some kind of "survival mechanism." After this discussion I began to remember occasions when I had been made aware that I was, in fact, something of a role model. These incidents provided the genesis of this book, which I hope will not only encourage young women to enter science, but maybe, along the way, it will also explain some particle physics to a broader audience, as well as the excitement of doing science, or just the fun of learning it, as I had the good fortune of having a career that spanned the remarkable period of the inception, in the late 1960s and early 1970s, of what is now known as the Standard Model of particle physics and its confirmation by experiments, culminating with the discovery of the Higgs particle in 2012.

The narrative below recounts my experiences as a woman in a very male-dominated field, while following the development of the Standard Model as I witnessed it and participated in it. The generally nurturing environment of my childhood and college years undoubtedly helped to shape my "survival mechanism." My experiences as an undergraduate in particle physics laboratories and as a first-year graduate student at Columbia University cemented my passion for physics. Nothing in the first 20 years of my life had prepared me for the difficulties that I would confront as a second-year graduate student in Paris, and later during my nearly 20 years at CERN, a laboratory now extending from the village of Meyrin, near Geneva, into the foothills of the Jura mountains in France.

The evolution of the Standard Model is described through the lens of my own work, in a language intended for a lay audience. As an undergraduate summer student at Brookhaven National Laboratory on Long Island, I first learned about the four fundamental forces of nature: strong, electromagnetic, weak and gravitational. In a discussion of my work on the physics of particles called "kaons," I introduce the postulate of quarks as fundamental constituents of nature. My work on charm at Fermilab with Ben Lee and John Rosner — including the successful prediction with Lee of the charm quark mass — entails a description of the now accepted theory of electromagnetic and weak interactions. Other work with Lee leads to an introduction to the present theory of strong interactions.

Discussions of subsequent work at CERN with John Ellis and others further develop these concepts. In describing my work on the Higgs particle (sometimes called the "God particle") with Ellis and Dimitri Nanopoulos, I explain why it is needed for us to be here to talk about it, and why, in its presence, the world we live in does not reflect the underlying symmetry of the Standard Model. An account of my prediction with Ellis and Graham Ross of the observation of experimental signs of "gluons" (the glue the holds the quarks together to form the particles we observe) further elucidates the theory of strong interactions. Some of my work with Ellis, Pierre Binétruy and others involved the interface of particle physics with cosmology; features of the evolution of the early universe are also described.

The description of the development of the Standard Model is accompanied throughout by accounts of the difficulties — and joys — that I faced in pursuing a scientific career while raising three children, and of the incidents of bias that I encountered. By the late 1970s my situation at CERN had become untenable for me. This led me to start a theory group in Annecy-le-Vieux, France, but not long thereafter I moved back to the United States, becoming the first woman on the physics faculty at the University of California at Berkeley. In the US I became very involved in service to the scientific community — including efforts to increase the participation of women in physics — as well as teaching and continuing research. This included Higgs physics, physics of the early universe and superstring theory. Although the Standard Model is a remarkable achievement, it is incomplete — in part because it does not include gravity — and some attempts to go beyond it, such as superstring theory, are again described through the lens of my own research.

I close with some reflections on attitudes towards women in science and towards science in general.

The account that follows is based on my own recollections, which may be faulty. I have tried to verify as much as possible (Wikipedia has been a godsend in this respect). Some names have been left out in places by discretion, so as not to embarrass the interlocutor in question, others simply because of senior forgetfulness (and no help from my Google searches). I apologize in advance for errors in my historical account of events.

I am grateful to the many physicists who befriended me and encouraged me. Those not explicitly mentioned in the text include Paul Musset and Pierre Darriulat, as well as countless others. I always had tremendous support from the CERN theory group secretariat, starting with Tatiana Fabergé and Marie-Noël Fontaine. They were so helpful that when

In New York City as a Columbia graduate student. Courtesy of David Balzarini.

I recruited Nanie Perrin, whom I knew as a family friend, to be my secretary at Annecy, they agreed to train her, but she turned out to be so good that they stole her from me. Sheila McGarry, with whom my daughter Dominique and I put up posters to announce what we hoped would be the opening of a full-day nursery school, and Suzy Vascotto were also wonderful friends.

My very close friends Nan Phinney, Kathie Hardy and Kate Morgan helped me through a difficult period in my personal life, without which help I might not have had the courage to make a major life change that resulted in the very positive, for me, decision to move back to the United States.

And my deepest thanks go to both of my husbands, who in their own ways did their best to support me, and to my three children who put up with, and sometimes even encouraged, a working mother.

Contents

Beginnings

I was walking home from school, up the steep driveway, towards the very large and very old house that we shared with two other faculty families. Before, we had lived in a very large and very old faculty house all to ourselves. I don't remember, or perhaps never knew, why we had to leave it. It was a lot more fun. It had once been owned by a woman who put a large vat filled with sand in the attic to catch an atomic bomb when it fell. She was perhaps not so eccentric as one might think — those were also the days when we had to practice ducking under our classroom desks as preparation for a nuclear attack. The sand-filled vat was still in the house — an attraction that my brother and I would escort our friends to the attic to admire. The bedrooms had built-in closets with large drawers at the bottom. My friend Eleanor and I would amuse ourselves by pulling out the closet drawers in adjoining rooms and then peering at each other through the open hole in the wall. My older brother George was convinced that the house was a station on the Underground Railroad, the escape route for former slaves, and I once caught him (and promptly told our mother) dismantling the fireplace to find irrefutable evidence for his claim.

But that was the other house. In our present house there was just one other offspring of a faculty couple, an older boy who was studying ant hills as I approached up the driveway. I must have been about sixteen years old. Maybe he asked me what I wanted to do in life, or maybe I just told him that I wanted to be a physicist. "A singularly unfeminine profession," was his response. I don't know why I remember this — perhaps because it was the first time someone told me I had no business wanting to be a physicist. I don't remember anything else about him.

1

His comment rolled off like raindrops from a slicker, as did other comments I received as a youngster — presumably an early manifestation of my "survival mechanism." The only other remark I remember as a teenager was offered by the mother of a friend as I was about to go off to college: "Too bad you can't get married and have children," because if I did I would waste the money spent on my education. These were rare occurrences in an environment where there was little to suggest that I couldn't do anything I wanted to. Nothing in my early life would prepare me for the obstacles I encountered when, as a second-year graduate student, I moved to Europe in 1961.

I had been christened Mary Katharine Ralph, my first and second names coming from my two grandmothers. My parents originally called me "Mary Kay," but soon dropped the Kay. I later resuscitated it, eventually as just "K," because I was much closer to my maternal grandmother, Katey Casey, an Irish Catholic with an eighth-grade education (who privately practiced her Catholic faith in the German Lutheran household imposed by her husband, George Wiedmayer), than I was to my paternal grandmother, Mary de Forest Ralph, a descendant of the fabled John and Priscilla Alden and a long line of pastors, as well as the founder of New York City, Jesse de Forest — a French Huguenot living in Holland who inspired the settlement of what was first called "New Amsterdam." He never made it there himself; his son Isaac arrived aboard a Dutch ship in 1637. No one could ever drink or smoke around my puritanical paternal grandparents, but to their great credit they were pioneers in civil rights. My grandfather Philip H. Ralph, of Cornish descent, built — literally, by hand — an interdenominational and interracial church in Florida in 1943, when he was a 72-year-old retired pastor. I remember my grandmother telling me that she felt obliged to inform me that, because of her heritage, I was eligible to become a member of the (very conservative) Daughters of the American Revolution (DAR), but she hoped I wouldn't do so. Another consequence of this heritage was that every year during the high school years of my brother George and myself, there was a film shown in class about American inventors, including our great uncle Lee de Forest, the brother of my grandmother, with the teacher embarrassingly pointing out that we were related to him. When Uncle Lee wrote his autobiography, he sent a copy to all the males in our family. My father, Philip Lee Ralph, protested, so Uncle Lee eventually sent me a copy, with the inscription "in the hope that you will actually read this"; I'm probably the only one among my cousins who actually did read it.

No doubt my survival mechanism was nurtured by my family; there was never any indication from my parents that they expected anything more from my brother than from me. My worst memory of elementary school is second grade. We had just moved to Painesville, Ohio, from New Brunswick, New Jersey. The year before I had been in a private school at Rutgers where my mother Marion was a teacher, and my father was on the university faculty. After some testing, I was admitted to first grade at age five because there was no room in the kindergarten. The school was so good that it took me a couple of years of Ohio public school to catch up with the level of instruction in first grade at Rutgers Elementary. When I was getting low marks in second grade geography — which I disliked intensely — my mother met with the teacher, who said "Don't worry, you have one bright child", referring to George. My mother, who had been in the school system and had access to confidential records, said she believed I had a higher IQ than my brother, and, checking the records, the embarrassed teacher admitted that the real reason for my bad grades was that I talked with the poor black girl "from the wrong side of the tracks" who sat next to me. My father was not so proactive, but he was always someone I could talk to about anything, even interrupting his work on a book; he would patiently listen to my account of the musical I had just seen with my friends on a Sunday afternoon.

My high school also provided a largely nurturing and encouraging environment. The math teachers were mostly sports coaches, not particularly versed in their subjects (a situation which unfortunately still prevails today in many schools), but they were dedicated and totally supportive. Our geometry teacher would assign problems and then spend the following class having the four of us whom he had identified as competent — two boys and two girls — explain the solutions in class. It was really a great learning experience for the four of us — I'm not so sure about the benefit to the rest of the class.

None of the women teachers were coaches — we had a separate female teacher for girls' gym — and all were in the arts and humanities.

As a consequence there was no female role model to point me towards a scientific career, and my interests at the time were eclectic, and largely reflected those of my family — especially of my older brother.

I already knew the Latin teacher, Ruth Weigand, from my days as a Brownie in elementary school. She graded our work on a "curve," defining half of my point score as passing. I suppose the rigid structure of the language made it as natural for me as the math classes. Mrs. Weigand was also the advisor for the student newspaper; following in the footsteps of my brother George, I worked on the paper's editorial board from my freshman year on. I fully expected to further emulate my brother by becoming editor-in-chief in my senior year. When my long-time mentor instead chose my classmate Jimmy Naughton, I felt deeply betrayed. Years later, during the Nixon/Vietnam era, I realized that Mrs. Weigand had done the right thing when I saw James Naughton's byline on the front page of *The New York Times*. But I quit the newspaper editorial board, and my best friend Carol Baker, who was the yearbook editor, created the position of "art editor" for me, which meant that I illustrated the book.

Besides art, I had interests in music, drama, and writing. I played the piano ("like an adult" according to our upstairs neighbor in the second big house) and the recorder. My friend Ruthie England, who played in the high school band, got me to perform a piece for the band leader, who promptly wanted me to join the band and play the clarinet. This was vetoed by my mother, who didn't want me traveling to football games around the area. (She also wouldn't let me join the cheerleaders.) Our English teacher, Phyllis Brooks, was also the drama coach. In literature class we regularly recited poetry and performed skits. I remember reciting "The Highwayman" and, with two friends, playing the witch scene from *Macbeth*. My first time on stage had been at Rutgers Elementary, where I had to say just one line: "Don't fence me in." I was so shy that during rehearsal I was almost inaudible and they considered replacing me, but they didn't and at the performance — where the stage lights hid the audience and I lost my inhibitions — I apparently belted it out with gusto. In high school we did the standard drama repertoire — including, appropriately, *Our Miss Brooks*. That same shyness hampered my performance in high school try-outs. I think I had a couple of bit parts, but more often I was prompter. Once, we were planning a junior high[1] (seventh and eighth grades) production — maybe it was *Our Town* — and Miss Brooks drafted my brother from senior high (grades 9–12) to play the lead. George, who probably inherited his acting ability from my mother, went on to a career of acting, directing and teaching drama. Shortly after the play was performed, we were driving to Florida for our occasional Christmas with my father's side of the family. To pass the time in the back seat, my brother and I recited the whole play, he in his leading role, and me reciting all the rest, which I had unconsciously memorized as prompter.

In college I occasionally played the piano for my own relaxation, and I took classes in painting and creative writing, neither of which I particularly excelled at. But by the time I got to graduate school my creative energy was consumed by physics, except for playing the recorder with a group convened by one of the professors, Jack Steinberger, until it disbanded when Jack turned to the flute he had bought for his son, who soon abandoned it.

The humanities teacher who probably had the most direct influence on the course of my life was our French teacher, Edith Hamilton, whose students regularly placed among the top in the state French competition. We spoke exclusively French in class and in French club, almost from day one, and the two-year course included an excursion to the town of Marietta, a French settlement in southern Ohio. As a consequence when I got to college I passed the French "exit exam" (exemption from the language requirement, usually afforded to those with four years of high-school language classes) and enrolled in a French literature class. By the time I got to Paris in mid-sophomore year, I already knew enough French to skip the basic language classes. One course I had involved attending a play a week and writing a review of it. I also attended math and science courses in Paris. So by the time I met Jean-Marc Gaillard as a summer student at Brookhaven, a National Laboratory on Long Island, I was already fairly fluent in French — considerably more so than he was in

---

[1]This was before middle school was invented, and our junior and senior components together comprised Harvey High School.

English, which probably had a lot to do with my ending up as his wife in France.

In those days we had to take only two years of science for entry into college. The choices were general science, biology, chemistry and physics, in that order. My friends Leon Lederman and Shirley Malcom, who have been active in promoting improvement in science education, have argued for many years that the order is backwards, and I tend to agree. Anyhow, "general science" sounded blah, and I couldn't stand the idea of cutting up frogs, which is what one did in high school biology back then, aside from drawing leaves, which didn't particularly excite me. So I opted for chemistry and physics. These were taught, not by a football coach, but by a rather crotchety older professor who told us (not without reason): "It's unfortunate that Fahrenheit didn't die before he invented his temperature scale." I didn't much like organic chemistry, but I tolerated the inorganic version, which was more quantitative. Finally in my senior year came physics, which I fell in love with. I'm not sure why, because it was classical physics, which I barely remember — I had trouble helping my kids in college when they called me with classical physics questions. I guess it was just because physics was mathy, with more meat, to my taste, then the purely math classes that I was so good at.

So I decided to major in physics in college. Not that I had any real notion at the time of becoming "a physicist." Women didn't become anything other than housewives in those days — although my mother, who was a teacher of English, speech and drama, a Planned Parenthood and school counselor, as well as an accomplished amateur character actress, probably provided a role model that I did not recognize at the time. I remember in my senior year telling a friend that I hoped I married quickly, because I had no idea what I would do with my life otherwise. This rather resigned attitude would soon be transformed into a passionate determination, once I had begun to taste the excitement of high-energy physics research at laboratories in Paris and Long Island. The lack of early female role models in science was more than compensated for by the absence of any indication that I was less able than my male counterparts — an experience that must have armed me against the unexpected hurdles that I subsequently encountered as a second-year graduate student in France.

Our family did not have much money. My father was a poorly paid history professor in a liberal arts college near Cleveland. He used to work in the summers to supplement his salary — once as a house painter, once as a milkman when he and my brother would leave early in the morning to deliver the milk — except for the summers when he had a grant to work on a book. Years later his very successful co-authored college freshman history textbook, *World Civilizations* (Norton, 1955–1991), earned him enough royalties for a comfortable retirement, but back then we were struggling, and my mother was always clipping coupons and looking for sales to clothe us respectably. So I went to the college that offered me the largest scholarship. Although the school was hardly distinguished for its physics program — with one physics major about every two years — by a serendipitous stroke of good luck, this turned out to have a profound influence on my career.

Hollins and Paris

The scholarship took me to Hollins College, near Roanoke, Virginia, and the beautiful Blue Ridge Mountains. It was a Proctor and Gamble four-year scholarship: full tuition (which in private schools included housing and meals) plus an allowance for books. I later found out that a mistake had been made; I wasn't supposed to have gotten such a generous offer. If not for that mistake, I probably would have gone to Bryn Mawr, which at the last minute offered me a partial scholarship. It also turned out that Hollins at the time (at what today seems to be a minuscule amount: $2000 per year) was the most expensive college in the nation. As a result I was plunged into another world: debutantes, high society girls who went to college — sometimes only for a couple of years — until they found the right marriage material. Times change, and many of my classmates have excelled in real life — notably in literature. I also found a few soul-mates there, some of whom have remained close (but not frequently seen) friends throughout my life. My first roommate was Jackie Silverman, who was responsible for my acquiring a Jewish boyfriend, because of her con-nections with the Jewish fraternity at nearby Washington and Lee University. She left school after two years to get married the summer I was scheduled to be in Europe. My only regret was that I missed the chance to be the maid of honor in a Jewish wedding. After that I roomed with Lillian Shepherd, who was my roommate in Paris, and later in New York, along with another classmate, Peggy Marshall. Peggy is the one I have been closest to throughout the years, especially since we both ended up living in the area of Geneva, Switzerland.

I had more in common with the teachers, who were more like me in terms of background and world view, than with many of my fellow students. First and foremost, there was Dorothy Montgomery. She was really "a physicist," having written papers with Robert Oppenheimer, for example, although I wasn't aware of it at the time. I probably didn't even know who Oppenheimer was then. I eventually learned from Dorothy that she had had a non-tenured position at Yale, and was let go when her husband died. She was offered a position at Columbia, but had two small children that she preferred not to raise in New York City, so she moved to Virginia. This turned out to be a fortuitous happenstance for me, because of the pivotal influence she had on the course of my life. Dorothy was essentially the physics department at Hollins; there was just one other physicist, Dick Garrett, on the faculty.

Which leads me to Paris. Aside from the scholarship, a Year Abroad program had attracted me to Hollins. When I was about to embark on this venture, Dorothy contacted people in Paris to get me into Leprince-Ringuet's laboratory at *l'École Polytechnique*; this was a group that had done important work in cosmic ray physics in the 1950s. There I scanned emulsion plates, looking for tracks from cosmic rays — particles that bombard us from outer space — made by their interactions in the emulsion. After I got back to Hollins, Dick Garret set me up me up with my own emulsion lab, where I almost started a fire with a cigarette in the wastebasket. By then Dorothy had gone off to MIT to work on physics textbooks. To replace her, Hollins had hired a lame "instructor," whose name I don't remember, but who was supposed to teach me graduate-level physics using a standard text on classical field theory, and who became very angry when I pointed out (in front of another student) his mistake in understanding the text. At our next meeting he came back waving a bible, proclaiming that it was much more important than the textbook we were studying.

By my senior year, I became very restless. This was not my natural milieu. For one thing, I had long resented having to go to chapel, as we were required to do, at least a certain number of times in those days. Right at the start, I did go to chapel with my Episcopalian friends, and was mortified at having the cleric in charge put something in my mouth. I had initially also tried to fit in with the social life of my wealthier classmates, but by my senior year I had become close to a small group of friends, who, like myself, were not satisfied with the surrounding atmosphere. My rebellious friends and I had been labeled "beatniks" by some, although we did not consider ourselves as such. Maybe it was because we had started wearing pants, which had been frowned upon if not at one time forbidden. Oddly enough, our group of friends became very close to the college chaplain, Alvord Beardslee. I think he was as happy to find intellectually, if not religiously, compatible companions, as we were to find a refuge.

Maybe I had always been a rebel. I remember, as a very young child, my Irish grandmother taking me to the five and dime store to buy me a doll. There were rows and rows of pink plastic dolls, and finally I found something different: one black doll, which I immediately wanted. I had a tug of war with my grandmother over this, but finally she relented. I can't imagine that at my young age this was an antiracist act on my part, but simply wanting something different. Just as in second grade, when we were asked to draw the symbol of a country, I immediately picked the Soviet hammer and sickle — not because my parents were socialists (which they were, but they had always been anti-Stalinists, and I didn't even know who Stalin was then) — but because I somehow knew it was exotic and quasi-forbidden. Probably that's why I eventually rebelled against the idea, prevalent at the time, that a woman could (exceptionally) have a career or she could get married and have children, but certainly not both.

Then there was Allen Calvin — whom we secretly called Alvin Calvin — kind of rebel himself on the Hollins campus. He was a psychology professor; my close friend Peggy was a psych major, and I enrolled along with her in one of his classes. He apparently recognized something exceptional about me, and urged me to transfer to Berkeley for my senior year. However the people at Berkeley advised me to finish my undergraduate degree at Hollins and to apply to Berkeley for graduate school. As it turned out, I was drawn to Columbia by the time I graduated from Hollins. I don't know what became of Allen Calvin, and I doubt that he ever knew that I ended up as a professor at Berkeley. But he did play a significant role in pushing us to question our surroundings and to want something more.

Being antsy as we were as seniors, my cohort of friends and I, together with Reverend Beardslee, were trying to find a way to racially integrate Hollins. I graduated a semester early, and, as far as I knew, the effort dissolved. After I graduated, I never donated money to Hollins (which I couldn't afford to do anyway for many years). Then years later, my friend Nelle Chilton, who had been active in sit-ins at the Ann Arbor campus of the University of Michigan during the Vietnam War, told me that Hollins had been one of the first college campuses to protest that war. I was pleasantly surprised and sent a modest contribution, along with a note explaining that I was not happy with the only-white faces that I saw in the alumni magazine. I received a thank-you letter pointing out that Hollins had been integrated several years before. For some reason, the alumni magazines that subsequently arrived in the mail included a healthy sprinkling of black students. Had they been hidden so as not to offend a different sort of alumna?

My (almost) last trip to Hollins was when I returned as a Columbia graduate student to give a chapel talk. I don't remember how that happened; probably it was arranged by my friend Reverend Beardslee, and I think it was about capital punishment (against). I asked my friend: "How do I end my talk?" Beardslee, who knew I was an atheist, suggested the South African expression "Go well," which I did use. Afterwards I heard reports that the Dean reacted badly: "She could at least have said 'Go with God.'"

To Paris and Back

A loud crash awoke me. Flowers were hurtling across the room — the flowers that my high school friends had sent to wish me *bon voyage* from the New York harbor. I was on the Ile de France on my way to my year abroad. I didn't know how to waltz, but a very tall and strong German literally swept me off my feet, and got me into the waltz. We arrived in Caen. I was awakened in the morning by a phone call, trying to understand the speaker's French, until I realized he was telling me in English that it was time to get up. That was the start of the year in Paris that must have influenced my life in many ways. For one thing I became fluent in French, which was a factor in my first marriage. For another, thanks to Dorothy, I was working in a premier physics laboratory, which made my transition back to the much less stimulating atmosphere at Hollins more difficult, but also strengthened my resolve to continue in physics. More intangibly, that experience provided a budding understanding of a wider world and different cultures.

In the summer of that year, 1958, we had a tour of Europe — including a trip to the Soviet Union — under a newly established cultural exchange agreement. Some of us appeared on two TV programs in a series called "Youth Wants to Know," filmed in Moscow — but aired only in the U.S. We were accompanied by our Dean, who was terrified all the time. My friends and I said outrageous things to the hotel TV in the hopes that we were being monitored. I'm the only person I know (aside from my fellow Hollins students) who actually saw Stalin's body, which was still in the Mausoleum at that time.

Our summer trip also took us to a mountaintop somewhere in Austria, which we got to in a ski lift cabin. By that time I had become good friends with Nelle Ratree (now Chilton), a friend of my roommate Lillian, who came from a very wealthy family in West Virginia. She was a year behind us at Hollins, but her family had agreed to fund her to join us on the summer tour. Both of us being adventurous, we chose to walk back down the mountain, which had been approved by our faculty escorts, but being even more adventurous we decided to see what the other side of the mountain looked like. So we walked down the wrong side of the mountain, ending up in a village far from where we were supposed to be. We took a train back to the place where our group was staying, arriving around midnight, and incurred (not for the last time) the outrage of the Dean. That trip also led to my first experience with skiing. While in Innsbruck we met some Austrians, including a good-looking young man who fell in love with me, and who invited some of us to go skiing at winter break. That amounted to walking up a short stretch of the Austrian Alps and then skiing down. At least it got us broken in. My next attempts were on a small hill in Ohio, where there was a tow rope to pull us up. Then when I was a graduate student at Columbia, I skied at Stowe, Vermont, with real ski lifts (and a blanket to keep you from freezing to death on the way up), snow-plowing all the way down. But eventually in Europe I became a reasonably accomplished skier, and it was the one sport I really enjoyed until my legs developed problems when I was in my late sixties.

In the spring of 1958, just about the time our cohort was scheduled to go off to tour other parts of Europe, there were "black Marias" (police vans) all over Paris because of the events taking place in Algeria. Our college officials got worried and decided to get us out early. So off we went. Shortly before, I had been diagnosed with chronic appendicitis, and the British doctor at the American Hospital in the upscale suburb Neuilly that we had been instructed to go to told me: "If you were in Britain where medicine is free, I'd have your appendix removed." But as I was in Paris, where medicine was not free, he advised me to wait it out. So I came down with acute appendicitis in Geneva, and, after an operation, ended up in a boarding house with Barbara Zeldin, half of the faculty couple who were accompanying us on our summer tour. We had a very pleasant stay, with a bottle of wine that we kept for our table until it had to be replaced. Barbara was a Russian Christian by origin, and her husband, Jesse, was a Russian Jew. They were both philosophy professors who became good friends of mine during my remaining time at Hollins. I sometimes babysat for them, notably as the child carer during a faculty party they gave, at which I was also allowed to mingle with the guests, earning the comment from one hostile psychology professor: "I didn't think you were a member of the faculty yet." I think that he was resentful of the admiration that his colleague Allen Calvin had for me.

It was an interesting time in many ways, and the sight of the Blue Ridge Mountains often lifted my spirits when I got impatient with life at Hollins. Still, I wanted something more. I graduated mid-year and, at Dorothy's suggestion, applied to Case Institute of Technology (now part of Western Reserve University) in the interim, to make up for classes that had not been available at Hollins. That was something of a comedy of errors. First, Case replied that they had no accommodations for women — even though I had explained in my application letter that I would be commuting from home. I replied, reiterating my original letter and adding that I had been awarded, exceptionally as a junior, a (then prestigious but soon defunct) Woodrow Wilson scholarship that I would be using at Columbia University in the following fall. I got back a somewhat apologetic letter of acceptance. Dorothy had advised me to take courses in thermodynamics and classical field theory at Case. It turned out that the physics thermo class conflicted with the field theory class, so I took thermo with engineering students. I was of course the only woman in both. After the first thermo test was graded I remember walking past the teacher who was staring at me in utter amazement. A few days later, the teacher asked a question, to which I knew the answer, but being the lone woman and shy by nature, I remained silent. Then I heard a voice behind me hiss: "Why don't you answer him, *physicist!*"

The field theory class was more challenging, and in it I met someone whom I dated for about six months. I helped him with the material, and on the midterm we both got a B — in my case due to a silly mistake I had made, which I realized just as I was leaving the exam room. Then on the final, even though I was still tutoring my friend, he got a C and I got an A. But we both got a B for the overall grade, which irritated me. Years later the professor of that class was on sabbatical at CERN — the particle physics laboratory in Geneva where I spent most of the first 20 years of my career — and I was sitting near him at lunch. I mentioned that I had taken a class from him. Much to my embarrassment, he asked me what grade he had given me. I lied that I didn't remember. The next day (way before the era of electronic records) he came back with the — to him — sorrowful news that he had given me a B. I just shrugged. Besides being bemused by the fact that he carried those old class records around with him, I later regretted that I didn't tell him that I felt at the time that he had

Twenty-two years later: with Louis Leprince-Ringuet, circa 1980.

done me an injustice. Remembering such incidents makes me empathize with the shocking (to the women on the Berkeley physics faculty) revelations we are still hearing from women graduate students that they are intimidated by their male peers, and reluctant to speak up in class, group meetings and seminars. Is it something inherent to our nature, or is it that men are still insensitive? I have seen so many changes since I was a graduate student — confident successful women, younger male colleagues with professional wives, in physics or otherwise, and totally respectful of their female colleagues — that it is hard to believe that the experiences I had still persist, but apparently they do.

My very last encounter with Hollins was shortly after I had moved back to the US and was attending a meeting of the American Physical Society in Washington, D.C. I rented a car and drove to Roanoke to look up my old professors. I found a couple of faculty members who were impressed out of their minds that I was a professor at Berkeley, but of my old friends I found only Jesse Zeldin, whose wife Barbara had died.

Brookhaven and Columbia

Probably the best thing that Dorothy Montgomery ever did for me was to get me to apply for a summer student position at Brookhaven National Laboratory (BNL) on Long Island during the summers after my junior and senior years at Hollins. I was very likely accepted because of her influence and because of my experience in the Paris lab, which she had previously arranged. It was the Brookhaven experience that got me hooked on high energy, or particle, physics — and changed the course of my life. Nowadays it is standard for undergraduates aspiring to do graduate studies to get such an experience, often through the National Science Foundation (NSF) program called Research Experience for Undergraduates (REU). However, I frequently get requests from undergraduates to work with me on a theory project for a summer, for which I have no means to support them, and, more importantly, no work to give them at their level of expertise. I always advise them to try to join an experimental group to find out what particle physics is really about.

My first summer at Brookhaven, I was assigned to Bob Adair of Yale, but somehow ended up working with the Columbia group. However, the accelerator — a circular ring 72 meters in circumference, in which protons were speeded up by surrounding electric and magnetic fields until they acquired an energy of more than three times that of a motionless proton (soon to be replaced by a larger accelerator in which an energy 10 times higher was reached) — was down for repairs or upgrade, and there wasn't much to do. I spent a lot of time at beach parties, either with fellow students or with the Columbia group, but not doing much useful work. In the meantime Bob Adair was giving regular lectures to the two of us under

17

his tutelage (the other was a woman student from Yale), teaching us the rudiments of particle physics, as understood at the time. First, there were the four fundamental forces of nature, listed in the table below.

Force	range	strength	particles
strong	10^{-13} cm	1	$p, n, \Lambda, \pi, K \ldots$
electromagnetic	infinite	10^{-3}	above $+ e, \mu$
weak	10^{-16} cm	10^{-10}	all above $+ \nu$
gravitational	infinite	10^{-38}	all

The first column gives the name of the force. The second gives its range, and the third its "strength." Here "cm" stands for centimeters; the notation 10^{-3} stands for 0.001 (one thousandth), 10^{-10} stands for a decimal point followed by nine zeros before the 1 (one ten thousandth of a trillionth), and so on. The number 1 in the strength column for the strong force simply means that this force is unsuppressed: when two strongly interacting particles are in close enough proximity, they are almost certain to interact with one another. The numbers below it in the same column show the strengths of the other forces relative to the strong one, as measured at energies of about a billion electron volts, or over distances of about a hundredth of a trillionth of a centimeter. An electron volt is the amount of energy acquired by an electron traversing an electric potential of one volt. A billion electron volts is approximately the energy of a proton at rest: $E = m_p c^2$. Because of their infinite range, the electromagnetic and gravitational interactions govern most of what we experience in everyday life. Gravity holds the planets in their orbits and holds us on the ground. The electromagnetic force gives us light and radio waves, and holds our magnets on the refrigerator.

The presumed "elementary" particles known at that time were few: the proton p and neutron n are held together by the strong force to form nuclei. The electron e (or e^-) is bound to nuclei by the electromagnetic force to form atoms; the atoms are in turn held together by the electromagnetic force to form molecules — the building blocks of all matter. For example a water molecule, known as "H-two-O" (or H_2O) consists of two hydrogen atoms, each consisting of an electron bound to a hydrogen nucleus made of a proton and a neutron, and one oxygen atom, with eight electrons bound to an oxygen nucleus made of eight protons and eight neutrons. The neutrino ν (nu) is emitted together with an electron in the radioactive decays of unstable nuclei, a process induced by the weak force in which a nucleus turns into a lighter one. The weak force also plays an important role in the burning of the sun. The other known particles included the antiparticles of *p, n, e,* and ν, labeled $\bar{p}, \bar{n}, \bar{e}$ (or e^{+}), $\bar{\nu}$. Then there was the pion π (pi), a short-lived particle thought to be responsible for transmitting the strong force among protons and neutrons that holds the nucleus together, and the muon μ (mu), a heavier version of the electron, upon whose discovery, Isaac Isidor Rabi was prompted to query: "Who ordered this?"

There were also the so-called "strange particles," discovered in cosmic rays in the 1950s, such as the kaon *K*, a strange, heavier version of the pion, and the Lambda Λ, a strange, heavier version of the neutron. These were produced pair-wise in strong interactions, and decayed by weak interactions: that is, a short time after being produced, they disappeared, leaving behind a debris of the more familiar particles. They were named "strange" because their pair production implied a new quantum number (the term for an attribute of an elementary particle)

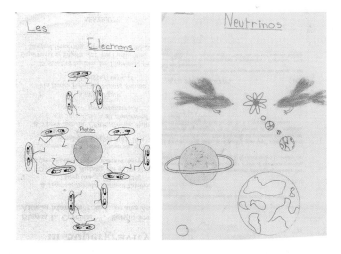

A (highly ionized!) hydrogen atom (left) and neutrinos (right) as imagined by Bruno Gaillard.

called "strangeness" that was conserved in the strong interactions; since the particles that make up ordinary matter carry no strangeness, the production of a strange particle like the Λ had to be accompanied by an "anti-strange" particle with the opposite value of strangeness.

This new conservation law was in addition to the conservation of electric charge in all interactions, and another known conservation law of nuclear physics, called "isospin," which means that the strong nuclear force is invariant under the interchange of protons and neutrons. This changes a nucleon into one of its "isobars," which has the same total number of neutrons and protons (collectively called nucleons), but not the same number of protons (or of neutrons).

I was always grateful to Bob for that experience. Very many years later he came to dinner at our house in France. After dinner Bob said: "I always knew you would be a good physicist; I didn't suspect you would be a good cook." It was the nicest compliment I ever received.

During my second summer at Brookhaven, I actually worked. I was again with the Columbia group, working on what was called the "cusp" experiment. I can't remember exactly what it was about — a strange behavior in the probability of interactions when the beam of particles hitting a nuclear target reached an energy that allowed some new process to occur. I don't recall that the experiment had a big impact, but I do remember that there was a great deal of excitement when a scanner[2] reported an event that had never been observed before: the decay of a Λ particle, produced in a collision of ordinary particles, into a proton, a muon and a neutrino. I caught the aura of excitement, but not the reason for it. "It's because you're not educated to understand it," said one of the senior physicists; maybe it was my friend Leon. That was not a put-down; it was a reinforcement, reminding me why I needed to learn more about physics. On the other hand, I also remember unwelcome comments that

---

[2] A scanner was a person who looked at pictures taken by a particle detector. The scanners were overwhelmingly women, referred to as "popsies" by an eminent British physicist in the 1950s. As it turned out, besides scanning emulsions in Paris, I ended up scanning cloud chamber pictures, bubble chamber pictures and spark chamber pictures in my summer student jobs. (I don't remember that my male counterparts were often assigned these tasks.) At least it gave me a taste of what experimental physics entailed in those days.

summer about "curves" when curious senior physicists asked me what I was doing (drawing graphs).

It was during my second summer at Brookhaven that I met my husband-to-be Jean-Marc, who was a "postdoc" at Columbia (although he did not yet have his French doctorate, which was a long procedure in those days), on the invitation of Leon Lederman. By the end of my first year of graduate school we had become engaged. Jean-Marc was scheduled to return to Paris by the end of the summer. I had enjoyed my year at Columbia. Although I was only one of two or three women students in classes of about 60, I had many friends among the male students who had been with me at Brookhaven. We sometimes studied together, more often with me helping them rather than the other way around, even though my physics background was sketchier than most of theirs — many of them had been undergraduates at Columbia. The first semester I did very well in the more quantitative classes, like mathematical methods in physics, taught by Gary Feinberg, and quantum mechanics, taught by Feza Gürsey, and less well in the more experimental ones, like optics and atomic physics. And then there was Shirley Quimby, who taught classical physics. His method was to fill all possible blackboard space before class began, and speak without interruption during the lecture hour. So we had to come early to copy the blackboard and furiously take notes thereafter. He assigned weekly homework that we had to turn in all at once at the end of the semester; this was returned to us, along with our final exam, with no comment or markings other than the letter grade for the course. His grading method consisted of looking only at the final answer for each problem, so if you made a sign mistake or lost a factor of two, there was no partial credit. I failed the first semester (rigid bodies — which I hated), while most of my friends managed to eke out a C. I was told by other faculty members not to worry, that the grade in that course didn't count for anything. My other struggle in that first semester was a required lab course that we called Lucy Lab, after the professor, Lucy Haynes, who seemed to have been doing this as long as anyone could remember. The lab equipment was not exactly state of the art; I mostly remember struggling to get oscilloscopes to work, and trying to make "eyeball" estimates of the errors, with Lucy telling me I was too conservative. The only session I really did well in was on the mathematics of error analysis.

And yet the culture had convinced me that I was destined to be an experimentalist, if anything at all.

I managed to get excused from the second semester of Lucy Lab, thanks to my two summers at Brookhaven. That semester I aced all my classes, including Shirley Quimby's (on classical field theory, which I loved and found very easy), so my confidence was growing. However, Jean-Marc wanted me to go back to France with him. I was enjoying my life. With one obnoxious exception, whose name I don't remember, my fellow students treated me with respect. Being hit on occasionally by a professor was just the way things were at the time; one learned to live with it. In addition, I wanted to stay at Columbia until I had finished the following fall semester of courses, so I would have a better grounding in physics, since I was aware of the rudimentary nature of formal graduate courses in France at that time. In the end, I was persuaded by people, such as Jean-Marc's colleagues Mel Schwartz and Leon Lederman, that I should follow my husband-to-be to France, with Leon (I think) talking about how I would be "self-taught, like all the great European physicists." I don't think he believed what he was saying, and neither did I, but that is basically what happened in the end.

In order to partially complete my master's degree from Columbia, which I needed in order to have the equivalent of a French university diploma, I took a summer class in statistics and commuted by train to Columbia's Nevis Laboratory in upstate New York, where I was working as a summer student. I took the class notes on a stenography pad, and studied them on the train. I remember a woman on the train asking me if I was training to be a secretary. When I said no, I was studying physics, she asked me, in a rather skeptical tone, why I was doing stenography.

Jean-Marc and I were married by a judge in Yonkers, New York, with my college friend, and New York room-mate, Peggy Marshall, and her boyfriend/fiancé Mimmo Zavattini in attendance. Like Jean-Marc, Mimmo had been brought to Columbia by Leon, and he and Peggy first met when Jean-Marc and I picked them up to go on a rock climbing trip with another Columbia professor, Jack Steinberger, whom I also knew from my stints as a summer student at Brookhaven.

We honeymooned in the south of France, and hooked up with Peggy and Mimmo along the way, because they were also moving to Europe–to

Geneva, Switzerland in fact, where Jean-Marc and I eventually ended up as well. At some point I got very sick from the unfamiliar food or microbes, while I was trying to study some thick physics book in order to pass an exam needed to complete the requirements for the master's degree from Columbia. This was an oral exam, and since I couldn't take it at Columbia, the powers that be had arranged (or so I was told) for a French professor to administer it to me, with details to be worked out later. I don't remember all that transpired, except that, feeling very sick, I finally called Leon and asked what was happening, and the answer was: "Oh, didn't they tell you? We decided to give you a master's on the basis of your grades." So I somehow got an actual diploma (in the mail I guess) that was duly deposited, along with my bachelor's diploma, in the depths of the University of Paris archives, after I was sent from window to window and was eventually told by someone behind one of the windows that I had to prove that my inferior foreign education was good enough for me to enroll in the French university system. I never recovered either of my American diplomas, and since the French University system doesn't award any, I have no proof of my education, except for a yellowed paper-bound copy of my Ph.D. thesis that I had to produce, many years later, as evidence that I was actually studying in Paris (and not spying, I guess), when I was being investigated by the FBI because President Bill Clinton had nominated me to serve on the National Science Board.

Paris Again: The Worst Year

Not really Paris. Orsay, a small village on the outskirts of Paris, near a metro station, but not much else. Although I was attending classes, I was also learning how to be a housewife, and was alone most of the time. I remember our friend Mel Schwartz visiting our apartment and saying: "She will make a great housewife." Not a very encouraging remark. Years later Mel learned better, when I had become an expert on kaon physics, and a consultant to his group at the SLAC accelerator at Stanford University. Once he was railing about a woman whose writing or advocacy he objected to, saying that she'd be better off staying at home and taking care of her children. His wife Marilyn asked: "What about Mary K?" to which Mel replied: "Mary K is doing important and useful work."

From home I had a longish walk to the *fac* (university). I guess we had only one car then. The other students all lived in Paris, so I didn't see them much, but a group with a car recognized me and picked me up along the way, and we became good friends. How did I end up with these classes as my only activity?

To digress, when I was a graduate student at Columbia, I had the impression that my professors didn't take me seriously. Not that they doubted my ability, but they figured that I might get a Ph.D., more probably not, and in any case would get married (which I did) and have children (which I did), and wander off into oblivion as far as physics was concerned. This also washed off me, as had my few brief childhood encounters with discouragement, except for one experience. I remember our orientation at Columbia. I was standing at the back of the room with two of my Brookhaven friends. The professor speaking declared that only one out of three of us would remain in the field. One friend and I instinctively looked at the other and said: "It will be you." As it turns out, we are all three still physicists in academia — and I am probably (or improbably from our vantage point back then) the most eminent. The other comment was that it is basically hopeless to think one could succeed as a theorist (the choices were theory, which meant mostly working with equations, on pencil and paper at that time, or doing experiments, which meant designing and working with complicated apparatus and analyzing data). It is well documented that women have lower self-esteem, so having been told that theory was beyond my reach, I assumed I would become an experimentalist, in spite of my private inclination for theory — I found myself much more at ease with equations than with equipment. However, while many members of the physics community implicitly or explicitly expressed skepticism as to my ultimate survival in the field, there was no question of being refused the chance to try, and judgment on achievement was essentially objective. I was soon to experience culture shock.

In the end, I became a theorist by default. Once I arrived in France, I did the rounds of the Paris labs, guided by my husband, who had many contacts, looking for an experimental group to take me on, since I was immediately told that theory was not an option, and most students joined a lab well before they obtained their doctorates. Bernard Gregory, at l' École Polytechnique, the premier French experimental lab at the time, and the lab where I had spent my undergraduate year abroad, told me I had done everything backwards: the correct path is to do undergraduate work in Europe and graduate work in the United States, and that I had come to France to get married, not to do physics. He offered me a job at a scanner's pay, and said that my name would not appear on any paper. I left the interview (once out of his sight) in tears. They all told me that they took students from only two prestigious schools (*Grandes Écoles*), École Polytechnique and École Normale, which were both all-male at the time. Finally, my husband's group leader Jean Meyer said he would take me in spite of his reluctance to have a couple in the same group. This was at a laboratory somewhat analogous to the Atomic Energy Commission labs in the US at the time, and I had to go through a medical exam. When I was asked when I had my last period, I joyfully responded: "I'm pregnant!" Well, that ended that job possibility because of "radiation hazards."

I never understood what they did about women who became pregnant after they had been hired…

Along the way, I also interviewed a couple of my husband's theorist colleagues. Roland Omnès said to my husband that he didn't doubt my ability *"parce que tu a dèjà acheteè la merchandise,"*[3] but he already had one student and didn't want another. Next came Albert Messiah, whose textbook on quantum mechanics was a bible at the time. (When I went back to Columbia, after a few months in Orsay, everyone there was talking about Messiah, with the standard English pronunciation, while I was using the French pronunciation "messia." By the time I left, it was reversed.) Messiah started by asking: "You couldn't get a recommendation from someone like Lederman, could you?" When I said "sure," he quickly changed the subject, and said I should go do optical pumping with (Nobelist) Alfred Kästler. When I insisted that I wanted to do particle physics, he said he would get a student of his to work with me, since, in the meantime, I had enrolled in graduate courses at Orsay. We had two study sessions together. We had a somewhat ambiguous problem from Louis Michel. There were two interpretations; one led to a trivial solution, the other to a more subtle one that required a lot of thinking. I opted for the subtle one, and my partner for the other. The next time we met he told me he had consulted a lot of Polytechnique students who emphatically agreed with his interpretation of the problem, so, being but a woman, I folded, and wrote up the trivial solution. Turns out I had been correct, and I ended the collaborative effort, figuring I would do better on my own. Years later, at the 1975 Lepton-Photon Conference at Stanford University, Leon Lederman was driving me through San Francisco to or from some event arranged by the organizing committee. I noticed Messiah at a street corner looking kind of lost. I mentioned this to Leon, who asked me if we should offer him a ride, and I impulsively said "no," although I later half-regretted my spitefulness.

The courses at Orsay that I remember were an impenetrable class on fluid dynamics that seemed to be included in order to give the professor something to do, and an equally impenetrable statistical mechanics class which consisted of lots of incomprehensible diagrams that I think the

---

[3] Because you already bought the merchandise.

professor (Loup Verlet) had invented. Then there was a straightforward, well-taught quantum mechanics course by my advisor-to-be Bernard d'Espagnat based on Messiah's text, and nuclear physics taught by the somewhat eccentric but fun Louis Michel.

I wasn't able to complete these courses, however, because we left for New York about half way through the academic year. Jean-Marc had arranged to go back to Columbia to participate in the final stages of the so-called "two neutrino" experiment led by Leon, Mel and Jack Steinberger, which was to become a landmark result. Along with two Columbia graduate students, Jean-Marc had participated in it from its inception, and even I, as a summer student at Nevis Laboratory, had helped to assemble apparatus for it, along with Jack's son Ned. And despite having to interrupt my studies, I was happy to be back in New York.

Since I knew I would have to pass exams in Orsay, I audited some courses at Columbia. One was nuclear physics, taught by Chien-Shiung Wu, who later won the first Wolf Prize in 1978 for her experimental confirmation in 1957 that parity (symmetry under mirror reflection) is violated in the nuclear decay of a Cobalt isotope. However, her course was hard for me to follow, so when I returned to France, I consulted a classmate about what to study to prepare for Louis Michel's nuclear physics exam. He told me to read a particular text — I don't remember what. I got through it and felt I had mastered all but the last chapter, which covered a very specialized topic that I thought surely wouldn't be on the exam. Well, that last chapter was indeed the subject of the exam. I lucked out on the other two written exams. (I seem to remember that happily we didn't have an exam on fluid dynamics.) One of the courses I audited at Columbia was statistical mechanics, taught by Quin Luttinger; it included a clear exposition of something called the "Ising model"; as it turned out, the Ising model was the subject of Loup Verlet's stat mech exam. The subject of the quantum mechanics exam was the physics of kaons, which was the precise subject of a class I had audited, taught by Jack Steinberger. It was a weekly class that lasted two hours, with a break for snacks in the middle. After class Jack, his new wife-to-be (or maybe his wife by then) Cynthia Alf and I would go to lunch at the cafeteria of the nearby World Council of Churches. Cynthia was a year ahead of me as a Columbia graduate student, and we had overlapped at Brookhaven. She was

Leon Lederman at the piano.

considered something of a sensation among the Brookhaven summer students because she had worked as model. One of the other women students (of which there were many, but mostly not in physics) told me a male student saw me walking outside the dorm and cried excitedly: "There goes Cynthia!", to which my friend replied: "No, that's just Mary K." I guess there was some resemblance. Jack and Cynthia later moved to CERN as well, and when I came to give a seminar at Columbia years later, I made a point of going to say hello to Feza Gürsey. He greeted me warmly and asked: "How's Jack?" I said that Jack was fine, and didn't bother to disabuse him as to my identity.

The French exam cycle included an oral exam that I handled well, in spite of my natural aversion to oral presentations (for a number of years I dreaded giving talks). I placed second overall in the exams and was accepted by the Orsay theory group to prepare a *thèse de troisième cycle* (third cycle thesis — the first two cycles consisting of the undergraduate university studies), which would procure a Doctorate equivalent to something between a Master's and a Ph.D. degree (and which no longer exists).

CERN

My husband Jean-Marc was offered a six-year staff position at CERN, in Geneva, Switzerland. So just a year after moving to France (and then spending part of this time at Columbia), I moved once again. We drove across France from Paris in separate *deux chevaux*, with baby Alain parked in the back seat of mine. Again relying on my husband's connections, I got a basement office where there were up to five residents at a time. I shared it variously with such luminaries as J. M. Jauch and E. C. G. Stückelberg (and his dog), as well as other young hangers-on like myself: Cecilia Jarlskog, Jacques Soffer and his wife, and maybe others that I don't remember. I also got the chance to work with Antonio Stanghellini, an extremely nice Italian theorist who was teaching me about resonances; these are strongly interacting particles that rapidly decay into lighter hadrons; "hadron" — from the Greek word for thick or heavy — is the name for strongly interacting particles like the proton, neutron and pion, and their strange counterparts. Unfortunately, Stanghellini died three months after I started working under his tutelage. Since I was nominally enrolled as a student in Orsay, Bernard d'Espagnat, a professor there who was on leave at CERN, agreed to take me on as his thesis student. This was perhaps a fortunate turn of events, because it got me into weak interactions, the area where I first made a mild mark.

The non-conservation of a quantum number, known as *CP*, was discovered in 1964 by James Christensen, James Cronin, Val Fitch and René Turley. This was a totally unexpected result. The *C* stands for charge conjugation, which means turning particles into their antiparticles, and the *P* stands for parity, which, in just two spatial dimensions, is the same as reflection in a mirror: under the parity operation the directions of particles are reversed. It had long been thought that nature was strictly invariant under the *C* and *P* operations separately, but in the 1950s it was discovered that both are violated in the weak interactions. However it was still thought that the product of the two was an invariance of nature. That idea was upset by the discovery by Christensen *et al.*

In their Nobel Prize-winning paper in 1957, T. D. Lee and C. N. Yang addressed an apparent puzzle in the decays of kaons by suggesting that nature was not invariant under parity and charge conjugation separately, but that *CP* was still conserved. There followed a flurry of experimental activity, starting with C. S. Wu's discovery of parity violation in Cobalt decay, and after the dust settled, the Lee–Yang proposal, that *C* and *P* were separately violated in weak interactions while *CP* was conserved, had been confirmed by many other experiments studying weak decays. However the result of Christiansen *et al.* showed that *CP* was violated a few times out of a thousand in the decays of kaons into two pions. Since no other sign of *CP* violation turned up until many years later, and its origin remained a puzzle, the leaders of the experiment, Jim Cronin and Val Fitch, were awarded the Nobel Prize only in 1980, after it was understood (see box on page 98) that the non-conservation of *CP* is a necessary condition for our being here to talk about it.

My thesis advisor, Bernard d'Espagnat, and another French theorist, Claude Bouchiat, were in my office discussing whether there was some way to test *CP* violation in different kaon decays. After they left, I somehow figured out a way to do it. This was one of my first papers. No *CP* violation was observed in the decays I studied, but it marked the beginning of my gaining some respect and reputation in France and in the world. It was in fact flattering that the paper was actually plagiarized. The plagiarized version turned up in an article that was submitted to a journal and sent to a referee, who happened to be a CERN staff member, and he seemed to recognize the paper. It turned out that the "author" had plagiarized others — one CERN visitor said he heard his own paper being presented by this person (whose name I have totally forgotten) at a meeting of the American Physical Society.

That was not my very first paper. My first paper, the subject of my *thèse de troisième cycle,* which I finished just as my daughter Dominique was being born, was on methods for measuring properties of resonances, such as their spin (the rotational motion of a particle, which is like a little spinning top). This problem had been suggested to me, not by my thesis advisor, but by Jacques Prentki, who became somewhat of a mentor to me. I wrote my paper and submitted it to *Nuovo Cimento*, the European journal of choice at the time, and went on about my business. An old friend from summers at Brookhaven came to visit, and we were showing him the house that we were having built in the hamlet of Echenevex, in the foothills of the Jura mountains — a site now sitting over the Large Hadron Collider (the LHC), which is currently pushing the high energy frontier of particle physics. I was enthusiastically showing a fancy window to our friend when I fell into a hole in the first floor where stairs were going to be placed, landed on my back in the basement, and ended up in the hospital. When I returned, it was to find that Leon Van Hove, the theory group leader at the time (who went on to become a Director General of CERN), had held up my paper because of some nitpicking remarks. (I think I used "affect" instead of "effect," or the other way around. I am slightly dyslexic, and my spelling has always been miserable. My father used to answer my letters — we actually wrote letters in those days — with numerous remarks about my spelling mistakes. When I was a senior in high school we had an exam for a scholarship that consisted a lot in figuring out whether words ended in "able" or "ible" and in "ance" or "ence." I was convinced I had failed miserably, but somehow I won anyway, and had to decline because of the large Hollins offer.)

My paper was eventually accepted for publication, but that was my first encounter with Leon's determined antifeminism — at least that's how I interpreted it at the time, and I'm afraid I still do. When I got pregnant with my second child, Dominique, I was terrified at the idea of him finding out, even though I was not being paid by CERN; I was simply afraid I would be denied an office and access to secretarial and other services. Much later, after I had had a very successful year at Fermilab working with Ben Lee, and was then working with Dimitri Nanopoulos and Shirley Jackson on a project that was dear to Leon Van Hove, I would be walking through the halls with Dimitri, who was much my junior, and, without so much as looking at me, Leon would ask Dimitri how the project was going. Still many more years later, when I had become a professor at Berkeley and a major proponent for the Superconducting Supercollider (SSC), I was visiting CERN when Leon called me into his office to lecture me on why the SSC had to play second fiddle to the Relativistic Heavy Ion Collider (RHIC), which was a project proposed at Brookhaven, and in which Leon had a particular scientific interest. He was, I think, still trying to exert his power over me as a woman, as well as promoting his own pet project over what the US high energy physics community — and the Department of Energy (DOE) advisory committee that I had served on — had overwhelmingly endorsed as its next project. Unfortunately, Leon turned out to be correct, because the SSC was canceled after it was 20% completed, on schedule and under-budget, due to the arcane reasoning of Congress, the body that at the same time decided to continue funding for the much more expensive, and much less scientifically promising, international space station.

After acquiring a *Doctorat de troisième cycle*, I was admitted into the *Centre Nationale de Recherche Scientifique* (National Center for Scientific Research, or CNRS) at the starting level of *Attaché de Recherche* (Research Attaché). To earn my pay (which barely reached what I had earned as a Brookhaven summer student), I had to take a train to Paris, at my own expense, every two weeks to tutor students at the École Polytechnique (one of the many places that had denied me access as a graduate student). I took an overnight train that got me to Paris at 7am, when it was still dark, and proceeded to the home of my advisor D'Espagnat, who had graciously offered me hospitality. I don't remember exactly how long this arrangement lasted. At some point, after I had written more papers on weak interactions, and especially on kaon physics, and, in 1968, finished my doctoral thesis, I got reimbursed for these trips, and I no longer had to tutor, just participate in the lab activities. Eventually I was told that the lab in Orsay could no longer afford my trips, so I was able to stop commuting. My doctoral thesis was completed two months after the birth of my third child, Bruno. To my Swiss doctor's apparent disgust, I was proofreading huge lithograph sheets in the maternity hospital bed. The degree got me promoted to the rank of *Chargé de Recherche*, with — finally — a salary slightly higher than what I had gotten as a summer student.

During that time I was mostly working and taking care of the children. The first couple of years we rented places in or near the French town of

Gex across the border from CERN (which then was entirely in Switzerland). We found a housekeeper/babysitter from a nearby village, who was quite competent, but left for personal reasons after a year or two. The second was a young girl, who walked to our house in slippers, even in the snow. I would come home and find that Alain and Dominique hadn't touched their lunch. After maybe a week of this, I tasted the leftover food and found it loaded with salt. I asked the girl why she used so much salt; she said her mother did all the cooking, and she had no idea how much was needed (I wondered what she ate herself). So we looked elsewhere. By this time, we had moved into our house in Echenevex, which was located midway between Gex and CERN. By a stroke of good luck, we were approached by our next-door neighbor, the wife of a cobbler, M. Fournier, who was also the local postman, riding his bike up and down the hills of Echenevex, whatever the weather. Mme. Fournier became our full-time housekeeper and stayed with us until she retired, just before I moved to California.

However, this did not give me anywhere near the flexibility of my colleagues — or the nearest thing to colleagues, CERN postdocs, since I was the only student theorist. We had two cars; I left for work late after child care, and I had to be home at a strict hour, so the housekeeper could leave, well before Jean-Marc and my other colleagues left work. When Dominique was born, just 14 months after Alain, we were living in an apartment in Gex. I drove to work and back to nurse her until the roads got too icy. When Alain turned three we enrolled him in the half-day CERN nursery school, and a year later Dominique joined him. This meant picking them up for lunch and then driving them home. And later there were music lessons and more. I was generally diligent about these duties, but once when my third child, Bruno, was about eight or nine, I totally forgot about his music lesson in Petit Saconnex, a Geneva suburb not far from CERN. It was in the middle of winter. He waited in the cold and dark for a long time, and then, a bit scared, hitched a ride with an older couple who drove him to the French border. The customs officer called our home and the *au pair* came to pick him up.

Once, my college friend Joyce Neiditz came to visit. After work I picked her up at the bus stop outside CERN and drove her home with me. Jean-Marc was away on a trip somewhere, and when I got home I fed my children (and us), played games with them, read to them — what I regularly did. Joyce (who was unmarried at the time) said something like: "I guess you never stop working," which was maybe the first time I realized that. Not to say we never went out, which became easier when we later acquired an *au pair*. After we moved to the Geneva area we skied a lot on weekends, which I loved (with the downside that I had to do the laundry on weeknights and hang it up by hand until we finally got a dryer). Once, at our daughter Dominique's urging, we took a family trip to Greece. There were other family vacations, including several trips to Turkey, where my parents were living for some time. And our magnificent view of the Swiss Alps helped maintain my morale — just as the Blue Ridge Mountains near Virginia had done. In fact the view of the Jura Mountains on the drive home from CERN often reminded me of those mountains over the Roanoke Valley. We could hike up the Jura from a path behind our house, sometimes just taking the dog for a short walk, and occasionally making it all the way to the top.

Since Mme. Fournier did not babysit at night, we finally decided to get a live-in *au pair* as well. We initially had several *au pairs* who couldn't drive, and since public transportation was all but nonexistent, we ended up doing a lot of chauffeuring, so that they could have a social life. So we eventually made a driver's license a condition for employment, and bought a third car. For a number of years we had a series of wonderful *au pairs*, some of whom I still correspond with — and on occasion get to meet up with. However at some point the quality began to decline (perhaps because more possibilities were opening up for young women), and they frequently left after a short time. One Christmas, after our *au pair* had announced that she wasn't coming back after the holidays, my son Bruno and I were standing in a ski lift line. Bruno, who was about 12 at the time, suddenly announced that he didn't want any more *au pairs*. Neither did I, and so we didn't look for another. Alain and Dominique were pretty independent by then, and we arranged for Bruno to stay with friends who lived near his school in Ferney-Voltaire until I could pick him up after work.

As a consequence of child-care responsibilities, and the fact that I was in the daunting position of being the only student in the theory group, initially I didn't interact a lot with other theorists. Aside from a few papers with my thesis advisor while I was still a student, most of my early papers were single-authored. I did interact with my husband's experimental colleagues, so I naturally focused on the interpretation of experiments — except for my accidental foray into group theory. In 1965, while I was still a student, Milan Nicolić, who was organizing a summer school in Yugoslavia, invited my husband to give a course based on the experiment he was working on at the time, and asked me to repeat Jacques Prentki's lectures on unitary groups,[4] which I had attended at CERN. Jacques said that the proposal was ridiculous and that I should devise my own course. So I did, and wrote a course called "Unitary Symmetry and Weak Interactions," which however included an introduction to group theory that I had learned from Jacques. We had two children at the time, who came with us to Herzog Novi, and the CERN theory group secretaries babysat our children with delightful boat trips and other entertainment. That was the first of two or three stints I did at that summer school, one of which ended up as a textbook on weak interactions, for which I was a co-editor as well as a co-author. It was a solid textbook as far as things stood at the time, but soon to be outdated by events starting in the early 1970s. Around 1980, not long before I left Europe, Milan asked me to get all the contributors to update the book to include the modern developments. I started working on my own contributions, and eventually got one completed new chapter from Otto Nachtmann, but no others. At that time my whole life was undergoing major changes, and I eventually abandoned the project.

Meanwhile, I was continuing to work on kaon decays. There was a prevalent theory (which eventually turned out to be correct), that predicted the properties of final state configurations in the decay of a kaon into a pion and two "leptons": a charged lepton l and a neutrino. Here a charged "lepton," from the Greek word for "light," can be an electron or its heavier companion, the muon. The experiments at that time showed complete disagreement with the theory. I proposed an alternate theory to explain these results, as did Richard Brandt and Giuliano Preparata, who were furious when my paper came out before theirs. They responded with some

---

[4]These are the groups of transformations in any number of dimensions that change a particular state into another one, without changing its probability of existing.

very insulting comments, and Preparata (who later had a junior staff position at CERN) was rather hostile to me until our sons became good friends in school. However, I eventually came up with a better way to analyze the data, and wrote a short paper, and then a CERN report, with an experimentalist, Louis-Marie Chounet, and finally a review on weak decays of strange particles published in a highly regarded journal, with Chounet and my husband Jean-Marc, who was studying the properties of the decays of the strange counterparts of protons and neutrons.

By this time our understanding of the fundamental forces had replaced protons, neutrons, Λ particles, pions and kaons with their presumed more elementary constituents, dubbed "quarks" by Murray Gell-Mann, one of their inventors, along with, independently, George Zweig, when George was a postdoc at CERN and I was still a (pregnant[5]) student. The quarks were introduced to explain the quantum numbers — such as electric charge, isospin and strangeness — of the observed particles, including "resonant" states: states made of three quarks or of a quark and an antiquark that rapidly decay to lighter hadrons via strong interactions.

Another quantum number that needed to be accounted for is called "spin." Elementary particles are little spinning tops with their rotational motion measured in units that are half-integers or integers times Planck's constant $\hbar$, which is a fundamental constant of nature that characterizes the (small) distance and (high) energy scales where quantum effects become important. At very small distances and very high energies, the classical mechanics of Isaac Newton and the classical electromagnetism of James C. Maxwell no longer give accurate descriptions of nature; the quantization of rotational motion into discrete multiples of $\hbar$ is one example of the departure of quantum physics from classical physics.

Particles with half-integer spin are called fermions and have the property, known as the Pauli exclusion principle, that two fermions cannot occupy the same physical state. Particles with integer spin, like π, K with spin 0, and resonant states with one unit of spin, are called bosons, and are not subject to the Pauli exclusion principal. The quark model beautifully explained the observed states provided the quarks had half a unit of spin.

---

[5] I remember how convenient it was to rest the huge volumes of physics papers on my enlarged belly.

In this model the bosons are made of a quark and an antiquark, and fermions (like *p, n, Λ* with half a unit of spin, or resonant states with three half-units) are composed of three quarks.

If spin orientation is measured along a vertical line, a spin-$\frac{1}{2}$ particle's spin orientation can be up or down. Rotational motion is conserved in nature because the laws of physics are invariant under rotations in space, which can, for example, turn spin pointing up into spin pointing down. "Isospin" is conserved in strong interactions because the nuclear force is invariant under rotations in an abstract, imaginary space which turns an up quark (isospin oriented "up" in this imaginary space) into a down quark (oriented "down"), and vice versa.

However there was a serious problem with the model if one were to attribute physical reality to quarks, as opposed to viewing them as convenient mathematical constructs, as Murray Gell-Mann originally did.

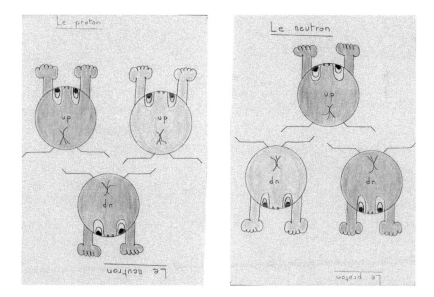

The proton, made of two up quarks and a down quark, turns into a neutron, made of two down quarks and an up quark under a rotation of 180° in isospin space. Courtesy of Bruno Gaillard.

The symmetry pattern that was the basis for the quark model had led to the successful prediction of the Ω^- (Omega minus), a spin-$\frac{3}{2}$ particle made of three "strange" quarks s with electric charge $-\frac{1}{3}$ (in units where the electron charge is -1), which was discovered in 1964 in an experiment led by Bob Palmer, Nick Samios and Ralph Schutt at Brookhaven. The possible spin orientations of the Ω^- include ones in which the spins of the three quarks are all oriented in the same direction. If the three strange quarks are just sitting motionless in an Ω^- at rest, they are all in the same state, which is impossible for three fermions unless there is some other quantum number that distinguishes them. This new quantum number, now known as "color," was first introduced in a 1966 paper by Wally Greenberg and Daniel Zwanziger[6]; if the fermions are all made of three quarks of different colors (for example, one red, one green, and one blue), the observed states were perfectly described.

There was initially some resistance to the idea that there were elementary particles with electric charges that were fractions of the electron charge. The up quark u has charge $+\frac{2}{3}$ and the down quark d, like the strange quark, has charge $-\frac{1}{3}$. No fractionally charged particles had ever been observed, and there were some attempts to construct models with integrally charged constituents of hadrons. But, as we shall see, about a decade later, the physical reality of quarks, as well as their fractional charges, was confirmed by experiments.

Radioactive decays of unstable nuclei can occur through a process called beta-decay when, for example, one of the neutrons in the nucleus converts into a proton by emitting an electron and an antineutrino. In the quark picture, this is interpreted as the conversion of a down quark d inside the neutron into an up quark u by emitting a pair of leptons; this turns the neutron, made of two d's and one u, into a proton, which is composed of two up quarks and one down quark. The decay of the positively charged pion π^+, composed of an up quark and an antidown quark $\bar{d}$, into a positively charged muon and a neutrino is now understood as the annihilation of the u and the $\bar{d}$ into a muon and a neutrino. There were also strange particle decays. For example, a Λ-particle, composed of one u, one

---

[6]The color quantum number had been anticipated by Greenberg in 1964 in the form of "para-statistics," according to which quarks behaved partly like fermions and partly like bosons.

d and one *s*, can decay to a proton, an electron and an antineutrino. This happens when the strange quark *s* in the Λ converts to a proton by emitting the two leptons. The decay of a positively charged kaon K^+ into a positively charged muon and a neutrino results from the annihilation of its components, a *u* and an antistrange quark $\bar{s}$, into the lepton pair.

Weak interactions had also been observed in neutrino collisions with ordinary matter, such as "inverse beta-decay," where a neutrino initiates an interaction rather than appearing as the product of a decay. A neutrino colliding with a neutron can convert it to a proton by turning into an electron, or an antineutrino can convert a proton to a neutron by turning into a positron, the antiparticle of the electron. Indeed it was this type of experiment that showed in 1962 that the neutrinos emitted together with an electron were distinct from those emitted with a muon. Starting with a beam of antineutrinos emitted in the decays of pions into muon and antineutrino pairs, neither of the above two inverse beta-decay processes were observed, but about 50 events were observed with a μ instead of an electron among the particles created in the interaction. This experiment, which provided the doctoral thesis material for three students, including my husband Jean-Marc, and the 1988 Nobel Prize for the leaders of the experiment, Leon Lederman, Mel Schwartz and Jack Steinberger, established the existence of two distinct neutrinos. The neutrino-induced interactions are now interpreted as arising from neutrino-quark collisions.

So by the end of the 1960s, the picture of the four forces had become:

Force	Matter	Mediator
Strong	*uuu*, *ddu*, *sss*	?
Electromagnetic	above + e, μ	γ
Weak	all above + ν_e, ν_μ	?
Gravitational	all	h

A photon γ (gamma) is a quantized bit of electromagnetic field; a ray of light is a beam of photons traveling with an energy of about a fifth of an electron volt. In quantum physics the attractive force between two "matter" particles of opposite charge, as well as the repulsive force between two particles of the same charge, is attributed to the exchange of photons between the particles. The photons are said to be the "mediators" (or "force carriers") of the electromagnetic force. Similarly, in the quantum version of gravity, the attractive force between massive objects is attributed to the exchange of gravitons *h*–quantum bits of the gravitational field. Unlike "matter" particles, these "mediators" are their own antiparticles. Both of these mediators are massless, which accounts for the infinite range of the electromagnetic and gravitational forces. A rule known as "Heisenberg's uncertainty principle" limits the distance r that the mediators can travel, and thus the range of the force, to be less than $r = \hbar/mc$, where m is the mass (heaviness or weight) of the mediator, c is the speed of light, and $\hbar$ is Planck's constant introduced earlier; when the mass m vanishes the range of the force is infinite. However, unlike the quantum theory of electromagnetism, known as quantum electrodynamics (QED), which is well understood and has been tested to very high precision, the full quantum theory of gravity has yet to be formulated.[7] On the other hand the gravitational force is too weak to be relevant at the energies probed by accelerators and colliders. Colliders — with two beams of particles circulating in opposite directions, that smash together at various points around the ring — provide more bang for the buck than accelerators, because all of the energy in the beams can be converted to mass: $E = mc^2$.

The issue at stake in the decay of a kaon into a pion, a charged lepton and its associated antineutrino was whether or not the up, down and strange quarks were much lighter than the bound states — protons, neutrons, pions and so on — that they formed, in which case the strong interactions had an additional symmetry, called chiral symmetry.

> *A "chiral" symmetry involves operations on massless fermions. A massless particle has only two possible spin orientations: parallel to its direction of motion (right-spinning, like the motion of a right-handed screw) or antiparallel (left-spinning). These form two disconnected states, because a massless particle always travels at the speed of light, so it can never be brought to rest. Chiral symmetry operations act differently on right- and left-spinning fermions. In contrast, a massive particle can be brought to rest, so its spin orientation can easily be rotated; all its possible spin directions know about the others, and they cannot transform independently from one another.*

---

[7]A current popular candidate for this theory is superstring theory.

The prevailing theory, with very light quarks, made predictions for low energy processes such as the kaon decay that I was studying. The configurations of the final state particles in this decay were governed by two parameters that had been chosen in a somewhat arbitrary way, and whose measurements were highly correlated. What Chounet and I pointed out was that a different set of parameters were uncorrelated because they measured the rate of decay into two physically distinct dilepton states. The parameter that governs the decay rate into one of these states directly probes the ratio m_u/m_s of the up and strange quark masses. Since their mass *difference* was thought to be about a fifth of the proton mass, if this ratio were close to zero, as predicted by the prevailing theory, it meant that the quarks were much lighter than the bound states they formed, with ms roughly a fifth of the proton mass m_p, and m_u much smaller than m_s. In this case some new phenomenon (now known as "confinement") had to be invoked to prevent the bound states (protons and neutrons, as well as pions and the strange counterparts of both) from rapidly disintegrating into quarks, which were never observed as free particles, except in one or two experiments that turned out to have spurious results. The experiments instead indicated that this ratio was close to one, which meant that the quarks were heavier than their bound states, with m_s and m_u both much larger than m_p. With new data, analyzed in terms of the uncorrelated parameters that Chounet and I had suggested, the prevailing theory, which was a step towards the formulation of quantum chromodynamics (QCD), now the accepted theory of the strong interactions, was soon proven to be correct by an experiment led by Stan Wojcicki at Stanford.

My work on kaon decays gained me some recognition. My friend and mentor Jacques Prentki appointed me as a scientific secretary, along with the young German experimentalist Konrad Kleinknecht, for the session on weak interactions at the Vienna International Conference on High Energy Physics in 1968. This was considered something of an honor for young physicists. A year later I was a scientific secretary at a conference on weak interactions held at CERN, and even had a discussion remark of mine included in the proceedings. I also gave talks at various conferences, which evolved from blackboard talks to talks on revolving transparent plastic that one scribbled on and cranked around as one spoke, to — finally — talks prepared beforehand on stationary transparencies.

Then in 1972, I was asked to organize a session on weak interactions at the very important biannual International Conference on High Energy Physics (ICHEP) at Fermilab in Batavia, Illinois. I also gave invited talks on kaons at a workshop in Daresbury, England, and at a winter school in Moriond, France. The following year I was invited to speak at another winter school in Schladming, Austria. The organizers didn't have sufficient funds to pay all the speakers, so they asked CERN to fund the speakers from CERN (as well as the students from CERN, which is normal practice). The theory group leader at the time — no other than my future husband Bruno Zumino — initially refused to fund anyone from the group on the grounds that it was all play (skiing), and no work (serious physics). But Bruno finally backed down when the director of the school insisted that he had to send (Nobel Laureate) Murray Gell-Mann and "Madame Gaillard." That was the school where I was dancing at a party with a young physicist. When I told him my name he started literally shaking with excitement, and told me he would get his coat and walk me back to my hotel. I took advantage of his absence to make a quick exit and go home by myself. It was also the conference where I became good friends with Bruno Zumino's longtime collaborator, Julius Wess, and where I leaned to ski with much more ease — skiing with a colleague without the pressure to compete that I sometimes felt with family. The next time I skied with Jean-Marc and Alain, they stopped to wait for me and were astonished when I showed up right behind them.

As for the basement office, as the years progressed and my work became more prominent, I rose up the floors of the theory division, promoted to offices shared with just one other theorist, generally a postdoc or a visitor. Finally I made it to the theory top floor with an office all to myself. But that was after I became famous for my work on charm with Ben Lee and Jon Rosner. I saw many CERN Fellows (postdocs) come and go, some considered good enough to be offered six-year junior staff appointments (and a few were offered permanent senior staff positions), but I had never been considered for any position. At some point Jacques volunteered the (unsolicited) explanation that they could not consider me for a six-year appointment because I would have had to leave at the end of it. This was a bit odd; we had come to CERN because my husband Jean-Marc had been offered exactly that. At the end of the appointment he took a (much lower-paying) position at the CNRS, like my own, but he never left CERN and had an office there until his retirement. There were many other people who had positions elsewhere but were physically at CERN.

Fermilab

I'm not sure how it happened. I was desperate to spend some time away from CERN, where I was increasingly uncomfortable with my status. We had spent a month or two at Rutherford Lab in England, where I was invited to give several talks on my work on kaons. Those were a happy couple of months. I also wanted a longer visit to my home country than the one or two months we had been there on a few occasions since my move to Europe. Then one day we were having lunch at CERN with Leon Lederman, and I think he suggested that we spend a year at Fermilab. He wasn't the director then; it was Bob Wilson. Perhaps it helped that Jean-Marc and I had both been session organizers at the ICHEP conference that was held at Fermilab the previous summer. So, after my coaxing Jean-Marc somewhat, we took off for a year in the States, which turned out to be a pivotal point in my life. Fermilab was a very new, and still unfinished, laboratory when we arrived. Our offices were in barracks, and I remember trudging through the snow to lunch with my friend Shirley Ann Jackson, who was a postdoc there (and is now president of Rensselaer Polytechnic Institute (RPI), but that's another story, remarkable in its own right). At some point during that year the "high-rise" was completed, and we moved in. At first Bob Wilson had insisted that there would be no closed offices, only cubicles, but the theorists revolted, insisting that they needed quiet private offices. So these were finally provided, except for students and postdocs. Even these were somewhat less than private. Through the wall, I reluctantly heard many phone conversations my neighbor had with his new wife — I particularly remember one about her choice of a hairdryer. There was a fledgling theory group, with Ben Lee as director, some

Some members of Fermilab's theory group in 1974. From left to right, Benjamin Lee, Mary K. Gaillard, Shirley Ann Jackson and Tony Pagnamenta. From *Fermi News*, Vol. 25 (2002).

postdocs and mostly visitors like myself. By then I had garnered some reputation for my work on kaon physics, and I was frequently invited to give talks around the country. So frequently that my son Alain, in seventh grade at the time, remarked: "You seem to be more famous here than in France," an observation that occasioned some reflection on my part.

This was a time when particle physics was in a state of flux. There had been a period of gathering experimental data, with theorists somewhat floundering about how to interpret it. There was now a proposed theory of weak interactions, revived by Steve Weinberg, and relying on earlier work by himself and by Abdus Salam and J. C. Ward (and partially anticipated in Shelly Glashow's Ph.D. thesis), which experimentalists were scurrying to check. What they were looking for was something called "neutral currents." This requires some explanation.

The reason for the success of QED and the failure of a quantum theory of gravity is that the former is a well-defined theory in the sense that all the predictions of the theory can be calculated and hopefully verified (successfully so in the case of QED) in terms of a few measured parameters, such as the electron mass and its electric charge. This was not the case for gravity, nor for the weak interactions as originally formulated by Enrico

Fermi with his postulate of a direct interaction, or "coupling" — at a single point in space and time — among four matter fields (p, n, e, ν, or in more modern parlance, u, d, e, ν_e). Because the Fermi coupling is very weak, the theory gave a good description of nature as a classical theory — as does gravity: quantum effects involve multiple interactions and therefore higher powers of the small coupling strengths, and could be ignored. However, if you actually tried to calculate these effects using the rules of quantum mechanics, you got nonsense.

This lacuna led to the conjecture of two mediators for the weak interactions, first called W^+ and W^- by Lee and Yang, which made the theory more manageable, but not really fully consistent. The reason two mediators were needed, one the antiparticle of the other, was that, in all of the weak interaction processes observed involving both hadrons, n, p,... (or equivalently the quarks u, d, s), and leptons, e, μ, ν_e, ν_μ, there was a net exchange of one unit of electric charge between the hadrons and the leptons. These interactions were dubbed "charged current" interactions. What the new theory — also called the GWS theory for Glashow, Weinberg and Salam, who won the 1979 Nobel Prize for it — achieved was the status of mathematical consistency, at the cost of predicting the so-called neutral currents, that is, the prediction of scattering processes that did not change the electric charge of the hadrons or the leptons, such as a neutrino collision with a nucleon (i.e., with a quark), leaving the electric charges of the quark and the neutrino unchanged. In the GWS theory these neutral current processes were mediated by an additional, electrically neutral boson called Z.

The experimentalists found the neutral currents, then they unfound them, depending on the experiment, so we started to refer to them as "alternating neutral currents." In order to make sense, from a theoretical point of view, the GWS theory required a new quark c, with the same electric charge as u, called "charm," a term coined by James Bjorken and Shelly Glashow in a 1964 paper proposing a new quantum number of that name (and presciently anticipating its important role in weak interactions). The new quark was needed to cancel a large contribution to the decay of an electrically neutral kaon K^0 (a bound state of s and $\bar{d}$ or of d and $\bar{s}$) to a pair of oppositely charged muons ($\mu^+\mu^-$), which was predicted by the theory, but was highly suppressed in nature.

Charm

At the time, the accepted theory of charged current interactions postulated that the down quark d decays into an up quark u, a charged lepton and its antineutrino about 20 times more often than the strange quark s does. This is called the "Cabibbo theory" because in 1963 Nicola Cabibbo first showed that the data on hadron decays with a charged lepton and a neutrino among its decay products agreed in detail with this postulate. However, there can also be processes with *two* weak transitions where an up quark emitted by a strange quark can turn back into a down quark, giving a net change of strangeness with no change in the quark electric charge.

In 1970, Glashow, together with John Iliopoulos and Luciano Maiani (GIM), had revived the charm hypothesis to address the observed absence of these "strangeness changing neutral current" (SCNC) processes, which leave the quark electric charge unchanged but not its strangeness. An example is the decay of a K^0 to $\mu^+\mu^-$, where a down quark can annihilate with a strange quark into the muon pair. This was expected to occur from a double weak transition even without any neutral boson Z. However if the Cabibbo theory were directly generalized to include couplings to the Z in the way required to turn it into a respectable, well-defined theory, the decay rate for K^0 to $\mu^+\mu^-$ was predicted to be a billion times larger than the observed rate. (For this reason, Steve Weinberg did not include the quarks in his 1967 paper, which he called "A Model of Leptons.")

Then in 1972, Claude Bouchiat, John Iliopoulos and Philippe Meyer (BIM) pointed out that such a theory was not really well-defined without charm; multiple interactions can induce couplings of three intermediate bosons to one another that destroy the consistency of the theory unless the electric charges of the fermions and antifermions sum to zero separately. Indeed when charm is included we have two sets of fermions (u, d, e and c, s, μ) with the same electric charges, namely $\left(\frac{2}{3}, -\frac{1}{3}, -1\right)$. Since u, d, c and s each come in three different colors, for each set the sum of the fermion charges is

$$3 \times \frac{2}{3} - 3 \times \frac{1}{3} - 1 = 0.$$

Without charm, there would be nothing to cancel the charges of the strange quark and the muon in the second set, whose charges would sum to −2. So if the GWS predictions for strangeness preserving neutral currents turned out to be correct (as they eventually did, by now with incredible precision), charm had to be taken seriously, because without it the theory made no sense beyond the lowest order in the number of interactions.

The GIM mechanism for the suppression of strangeness changing neutral currents requires that the charmed quark c mirrors the up quark u in that it decays about 20 times more often into a strange quark than it does into a down quark. The way it works is that 1) the rules for constructing a fully consistent theory prevent SCNC from occurring at the classical level (i.e., in the absence of higher order effects like double weak transitions) when charm is present, and 2) the charm and up quark contributions to the higher-order SCNC would exactly cancel one another if these quarks had identical masses. As a result, the probability of SCNC processes to occur depends on these masses.

But then, I asked Ben, why is the decay of a neutral kaon into two photons not suppressed? This decay preserves the quark electric charge, but not its strangeness, so the same cancellation mechanism should be in play. However the observed decay rate was similar to that of other weak decays involving photons that were not subject to the GIM mechanism because there was no change of strangeness. For about 24 hours we thought that the GIM scenario was in serious trouble. As it happened, Jean-Marc and I had a dinner party that evening. When Ben arrived with his wife, Marianne, he announced to Jean-Marc: "Your wife has made a discovery." Alas, I had not made a discovery; the next day Ben came back with the observation, based on work that he had done in a somewhat different context with Joel Primack and Sam Treiman, that the GIM cancellation mechanism is much less efficient in the two photon decay than in the decay of a kaon into a pair of muons. (However the dinner party also included Bruno Zumino, who had come to Fermilab to lecture on a *bona fide* discovery called "supersymmetry," which is still the subject of intensive theoretical and experimental research.)

Nevertheless, my non-discovery motivated us to embark on a systematic study of SCNC kaon decays in the GWS model with charm incorporated. This led to what turned out to be the successful prediction of the charmed quark mass.

- From the highly suppressed decay of a kaon into two muons we learned that the mass *difference* between the up quark and the charm quark had to be much less than the mass of the *W* boson, which at the time was presumed (correctly, as it turned out) to be much higher than the mass of the proton, for example.
- From the unsuppressed decay of a kaon into two photons, we learned that the up quark mass had to be much smaller than the charm quark mass.
- Finally we calculated the (very tiny) mass difference between the two neutral kaon states in the GWS/GIM picture. We found agreement with the measured value for two cases: 1) both the charm and the up quark masses are much larger than their mass difference, which is about a billion electron volts, or 2) the up quark mass is much smaller than the charm quark mass of about 1.5 billion electron volts (in the system of units where $c = 1$, that is commonly used by particle theorists). Combined with the result from our study of *K* decay to two photons, we were led to conclude that the second case gave the correct prediction.

Our results also provided further support for the idea that the up and down quarks were very light as compared to their hadronic bound states, and converted us into true believers in the GWS/GIM paradigm.

Our excitement over our findings was slightly dampened when we discovered, before our paper was complete, that Ernest Ma had also considered kaon decays into two muons and into two photons. However he predicted a charm quark mass of approximately five billion electron volts. The reason for his overestimate was that he overlooked the fact that the rate for the two muon decay provides only an upper bound on the difference between the up and charm quark masses; the observed rate is consistent with the decay arising from a two-step process involving both the electromagnetic and weak interactions.

After our paper was published, we also learned that in 1973 Arkady Vainshtein and I. B. Khriplovich had published in a Soviet journal an analysis of the two muon decay and the neutral kaon mass difference, and estimated a *c-u* quark mass difference on the order of a billion electron volts. Being unknowingly scooped by Soviet scientists was not uncommon in those days, since few Westerners knew Russian and there was not much East–West communication back then. Even when the Soviets started publishing more often in English, their work was often overlooked in the West, not out of malice, as the Russian theorist Vladimir Gribov once put it: people never really *read* other people's papers, they learn about the work of others through discussions with colleagues, so direct contact was an essential part of communicating ideas and results.

The first talk I gave about our paper was at my graduate alma mater, Columbia University. I went there with some trepidation, because Nobelist T. D. Lee, a faculty member who had been on leave during my short time as a student there, would be in the audience. I had attended many a seminar with T. D. sitting in the front row, mercilessly confronting the speaker with objections. In addition, my talk was preceded by a sumptuous Chinese lunch, and I wondered how I, let alone anyone else, would be able to stay awake during the lecture. But the talk went well, and there were no interruptions from T. D., who had, in fact, made a constructive observation when Ben and I had discussed our work with him earlier at Fermilab.

Besides studying decays that led us to predict the mass of the charmed quark, we calculated the probability of decays that had not yet been observed, notably the decay of a kaon into a neutrino, an antineutrino and a pion. This is the most accurate test of the electroweak theory in kaon decays because it is essentially free of uncertainties due to strong interaction effects. By the same token it is the best probe for new physics beyond the "Standard Model," the term for the theories of the strong, electromagnetic and weak interactions as currently understood. However this decay is quite rare and hard to detect, and so the experimental limit on its decay rate remained far above the prediction of the Standard Model for much of my lifetime. Recently there has been an observation at Brookhaven that is compatible with the prediction, but not statistically significant enough to establish the existence of the decay. Hopefully, experiments at CERN will do so soon, 40 years after our paper was written. Since then our result has been slightly modified. Our paper, published in 1974, was written before the top (*t*) and bottom (*b*) quarks were imagined — except by 2008 Nobelists Makoto Kobayashi and Toshihide Maskawa, who pointed out in a 1973 paper, published in a Japanese journal, that the addition of these quarks to the electroweak theory provided a mechanism for *CP* violation. This did not come to the attention of Western physicists until a couple of years later, after the discovery of the tau (τ) lepton in the 1970s, which necessitated two more quarks to restore the necessary relation among electric charges. It later became an integral part of the Standard Model, and its specific mechanism for *CP* violation has been verified in recent years by the study of B-mesons, which are bosons that contain bottom quarks *b*. (Hadrons with integer spin, like pions and kaons, are called "mesons".)

The Delta I = $\frac{1}{2}$ Rule

Upon completion of our paper on kaon decays, Ben said: "Now let's solve *CP* violation and the $\Delta I = \frac{1}{2}$ rule." Well, we didn't get around to *CP* violation, but we did make a significant contribution to understanding the "$\Delta I = \frac{1}{2}$ rule," which refers to a puzzle arising from an observed property of the weak decays of strange hadrons into ordinary ones. The underlying processes for these decays in the Cabbibo model suggested that the difference ΔI (Delta I) between the isospin I (which, like ordinary spin, comes in integer multiples of one half) of the initial decaying state and that of the decay products in the final state should be equal to a half or three halves, with roughly the same probability for either value. The puzzle was that the experimental results showed that isospin changed by a half a unit most of the time, with the probability that it changed by three halves smaller by a factor of 400 or more. This led a number of theorists to look for an alternate theory where these weak decays always change isospin by half a unit. Electromagnetic interactions do not respect isospin; small effects from these interactions could account for the small deviations from the rule.

This was precisely what my thesis advisor, Bernard d'Espagnat, was working on when I became his student, and I worked with him for a while on a theory that accomplished this scenario by the introduction of neutral vector bosons that coupled only to hadrons. I even came up with a theory of my own (simultaneously proposed by Raoul Gatto, Luciano Maiani, and Giuliano Preparata) that did not require new vector bosons, but instead new quark interactions. However this general approach — the idea that violations of the $\Delta I = \frac{1}{2}$ rule arose from electromagnetic interactions — had a problem of its own: electromagnetic corrections were expected to give comparable contributions to isospin changes of three halves and *five* halves, and there was no evidence for the latter. For me, at least, the nail in the coffin for this approach was a paper by Bouchiat, G. Flamand and Meyer. Using the approximate chiral symmetry of the strong interactions (which also plays an important role in kaon decays into leptons, as discussed earlier), they showed that the data on decays of kaons into pions supported the hypothesis that the decays with isospin changes of *both* one half and three halves arise from the underlying quark processes of the Cabibbo theory, with negligible corrections from electromagnetic effects. This result confirmed the prevailing theory for weak interactions, but it also implied that strong interaction effects must be responsible for the predominance of processes that change isospin by half a unit.

The verification of the predictions of chiral symmetry was important on two fronts. It confirmed that the weak interactions arise from the couplings of *currents*, analogous to the electromagnetic current that couples to the photon (and that runs through your electrical wires). This in turn meant that the weak interactions could be attributed to the exchange of spin-one vector bosons between fermions. It further implied that the up and down quarks are very light, and that the strong interactions respect chiral symmetry, which means that these interactions cannot turn a left-spinning quark into a right-spinning one. A *mathematically consistent* theory requires that strong interactions among quarks be mediated by spin-zero or spin-one bosons; only the latter respect chiral symmetry.

Meanwhile, experimental studies in 1969 of electron–proton interactions at SLAC in Menlo Park, California, had shown that at sufficiently high energy the quarks inside the protons interact with electrons in the same way that muons do (up to the difference in the value of the electric charge), just as if there were no strong couplings among them. This observed behavior, which garnered the 1990 Nobel Prize for Jerry Friedman, Henry Kendel and Dick Taylor, was known as Bjorken scaling, since James (Bj) Bjorken had predicted its onset at *very* high energies, based on the properties of the electromagnetic current. The same predictions could be obtained by assuming that the constituents of the nucleons (called "partons" by Dick Feynman) were point-like elementary objects with spin $\frac{1}{2}$. The SLAC experiments, and subsequently the Gargamelle neutrino experiments at

The CERN bubble chamber Gargamelle: as imagined by Bruno Gaillard, on display at CERN, as seen by the camera.

CERN, confirmed the spins, electric charges and weak couplings of quarks, and they further implied that the strong interactions had to become weak at high energies (and short distances), a property called "asymptotic freedom," but strong at low energies (and long distances) in order to account for the confinement of quarks inside hadrons: the force binding the quarks together increases as they are pulled apart.

Consider probing a proton with an electromagnetic wave. The energy of the wave is proportional to its frequency of oscillation, which is inversely proportional to its wavelength (the length of a single oscillation). At low energy when the wavelength is much larger than the size of the proton, the proton appears as a point-like object to the electromagnetic probe. As the energy increases and the wavelength decreases, the probe can resolve smaller distances, and interact directly with the constituents of the proton. Because of the well-known wave–particle duality of quantum mechanics, an electromagnetic wave can be interpreted as a beam of particles (photons), and any beam of particles can be interpreted as a wave, so the same property holds for electrons and neutrinos hitting a nuclear target.

Thus began the search for an asymptotically free theory. In 1970, Gerhard 't Hooft (who won the 1999 Nobel Prize together with his thesis advisor Martinus (Tini) Veltman) had shown that a class of theories known as "non-Abelian gauge theories"[8] (see boxes below) are fully

---

[8] The name Abelian refers to the Norwegian mathematician Niels Henrik Abel.

mathematically consistent. This remains true even when the gauge symmetry is "spontaneously" broken, which means that the world around us does not display the symmetry of the laws of physics. 't Hooft's paper was somewhat opaque to many theorists, but most of them were convinced by a different proof from Ben Lee and Jean Zinn-Justin in 1972, which inspired Steve Weinberg to revisit his 1967 paper, proposing what became known as the GWS model, which provides an example of a spontaneously broken gauge symmetry. 't Hooft also found that unbroken non-Abelian gauge theories can be asymptotically free, but apparently was not aware of the significance of this property for experiments.

In the summer of 1973, David Gross and Sidney Coleman showed that the other known well-defined theories — for example "Abelian" gauge theories like QED, and "Yukawa" theories in which forces among fermions are mediated by spin-zero scalar bosons instead of spin-one vector bosons — are not asymptotically free. Around the same time David Politzer, and independently Gross and Frank Wilczek, showed that non-Abelian gauge theories *are* asymptotically free provided there are not too many matter particles.

A gauge theory possesses a symmetry under a group of transformations that act on particles differently at different points in space and time. The strong interactions are invariant if protons everywhere simultaneously turn into neutrons. However the electroweak theory has a gauge symmetry; an electron in your table can turn into a neutrino, while one on the moon remains unchanged. This enlarged symmetry requires one or more spin-one "gauge bosons" that mediate the interactions among matter particles. Conversely, a theory with spin-one bosons is not well-defined unless it has a gauge symmetry. An example of an Abelian gauge theory is QED, in which particles with an electromagnetic charge interact via the "mediator," which in this case is the photon. In non-Abelian gauge theories, the mediators also carry charge, and therefore have direct couplings with one another. For example, the GWS theory is also called the "electroweak" theory because the W bosons, which carry electric charge, necessarily couple to the photon. The achievement of this theory, incorporating both the electromagnetic and weak interactions, is similar to Maxwell's unification of electric and magnetic forces into a single

---

(Continued)

(Continued)

theory of electromagnetism. In QCD, the color symmetry is "gauged," which means that there are vector bosons that mediate interactions among quarks of different color. Since color is conserved overall, this in turn requires that these mediators, called gluons (the glue that holds the quarks together inside nucleons and other hadrons), must carry color themselves, and thus interact directly with one another. Each vector boson in a gauge theory corresponds to a symmetry operation. For example, the photon of QED corresponds to multiplication of each electrically charged particle by a complex number of unit magnitude (see glossary). If one makes more than one of these multiplicative operations, the resulting overall change is the same no matter in what order the individual operations are made, and the theory is called Abelian. In non-Abelian gauge theories, as well as multiplicative operations, there are additional symmetry operations that change one particle into another (as in isospin), and the order of successive operations is important. Invariance under rotations in space is an example of a non-Abelian symmetry: just try turning any three-dimensional object sideways, then upside down. Now do the reverse order.

Rotating the stick figure clockwise by 90° in the plane of the page, then rotating it by 180° around the horizontal axis on the page (top row) gives a different result from doing these operations in the opposite order (bottom row).

In QCD, which had been proposed a year earlier by Murray Gell-Mann and Harald Fritsch, color symmetry is gauged. As a consequence there are as many vector bosons as there are operations that can change the color of a quark, or can affect quarks of different color differently. There are six ways to change the color of a quark: red to blue or green, blue to green, and the three reverse operations. There are also three different multiplicative operations, one for each color. One combination of the latter changes all the quarks the same way. The place where it occurs in a set of successive transformations doesn't matter, so it is not part of the set of non-Abelian symmetry operations. Thus there are eight gluons; in this case the theory is asymptotically free provided there are no more than 16 different fermion "flavors." The quarks are assigned two types of quantum numbers: color and flavor, the latter distinguishing the three colored up quarks from the down quarks and the strange quarks, for example.

In the spring of 1974, QCD was in its infancy. Asymptotic freedom had just been discovered. Ben and I had all but ignored it in our study of rare kaon decays, but Ben suggested that we take a look at QCD effects in weak decays of hadrons into hadronic final states. Our analysis showed that these effects indeed enhance the probability for changing isospin by half a unit.

Gluon interactions with quarks depend on the quark color, but are independent of their flavor: a gluon couples to an up quark in the same way that it does to a quark of any other flavor. So how does QCD know anything about isospin? It boils down to the Pauli exclusion principle, which necessitated the introduction of color in the first place. In the Standard Model, a strange quark can turn into a down quark when it collides with an up quark. According to the weak interaction theory, this process occurs only when the initial (s, u) and final (d, u) diquark states are symmetric under the exchange of the quarks' positions in space, and antisymmetric under the exchange of their spins. The diquark states must be antisymmetric overall; otherwise the two quarks would sometimes find themselves in the same state, which is forbidden by the Pauli principle. So if the diquarks are in antisymmetric color states they must also be in antisymmetric flavor states and vice versa. QCD collision probabilities depend on the color symmetry, which has to be the same in the initial and final states because color remains unchanged in all interactions. The initial state in the above collision process has half a unit of isospin, because the strange quark carries no isospin, and the up quark has isospin $\frac{1}{2}$. The antisymmetric flavor state for the (u, d) diquark has no isospin, so in this case the overall process changes isospin by half a unit. It turns out that strong interaction effects enhance transitions in the antisymmetric color state and slightly suppress those in the symmetric color state, which has isospin one in the final state, and contributes to decays that change isospin by both one half and three halves.

After we had finished our paper, we became aware of a paper by Guido Altarelli and Luciano Maiani, who had done the same calculation except that they claimed that we had left out a purely $\Delta I = \frac{1}{2}$ contribution in which a strange quark splits into a W boson and an up or charm quark, which then annihilate into a down quark. We quickly convinced them that this process does not contribute to the weak decay. It simply redefines what one calls a strange quark and a down quark because it happens all the time, as does the inverse process that turns the down quark back into a strange quark; one ends up with two quarks with two different masses that we identify as *s* and *d*.

However in 1975, Arkady Vainshtein, Valentin Zakharov, and Mikhail Shifman published, first in Russian in a Soviet journal, but later in English in a European journal, the observation that the same process with a gluon emitted as well is important because its probability is proportional to the squared inverse of the light quark masses. The importance of these contributions, now known as "penguins," was subsequently confirmed by more rigorous methods that had been developed to study QCD effects at low energy.

Although the contribution that Ben and I found did not by itself fully account for the observed $\Delta I = \frac{1}{2}$ rule, our paper remained influential because of the techniques we developed for treating QCD corrections to weak processes at low energy, techniques that have since been extended to the analysis of possible new physics beyond the known elementary forces and particles.

Search for Charm

After we had completed the K-decay calculations, Ben and I became convinced that charm had to be there. We decided to investigate in detail the ways in which the production of charm in particle experiments could be detected. Because we were more expert in weak interactions than in hadron properties and strong interactions, Ben suggested that we ask Jon Rosner to join us. Jon had been thinking about these aspects of charm particle production in accelerator experiments. This was the genesis of the "GLR" paper, circulated as a "preprint" (pre-publication version) in August 1974, three months before what has become known as the "November revolution", when two groups—one studying electron-positron collisions, the other proton-proton collisions—announced the discovery of a new particle weighing about three times the proton mass, just as we had anticipated for the mass of a charm-anticharm quark bound state.

I don't remember whether it was before or after we had begun our collaboration with Jon that I gave a "wine and cheese" talk at Fermilab that attracted a very large audience. Then in April of 1974, I gave a talk at an AIP (American Institute of Physics) conference in Philadelphia. Nobelist Richard Feynman gave the concluding talk. He said that it was appropriate that Ben Lee spoke about strangeness and Madame Gaillard (a name that he totally garbled) about charm. When, during my talk, my colleague Yaov Achiman had objected that I was promoting a theory with a total of 12 quarks (including color, which Achiman did not believe in, but which was accepted by the majority of the community), Feynman got up and said: "She's increasing the number of quarks by 4/3." After the session Feynman told me that I had given a very clear and precise talk and thanked me. (He obviously didn't remember that Jean-Marc and I had once given him and his young wife a lift in our *deux chevaux* to a conference in France.) Some years later I learned from my friend Val Telegdi that Feynman told him: "Maybe she didn't invent charm, but she explained it to me."

As for Achiman, I certainly bear him no animosity. After I had moved to Berkeley and was leaving Jerusalem from a winter school where my husband, Bruno Zumino, gave a course and I a lecture, I was stopped by the baggage checkers. I was afraid that they would ask me to open my bags and find the Israeli army caps that I had bought for my sons. But no, they were only interested in my airline ticket which had been issued from Jerusalem, and that took me there from San Francisco via Chicago and Rome (I must have had a meeting at Fermilab in between, and we were in

Rome to visit Bruno's mother) with a passport that had been issued in Geneva. This was taking place shortly after an attack targeting the Israeli airline El Al at the Rome airport, just about the time we left Rome (which had my mother wondering if she was seeing my boots on the airport floor when she was watching TV reports). I explained to the woman who had rudely stopped me that I had attended the winter school, but when I told her the place where I had stayed, along with the other lecturers, she objected that that was not where the students had stayed. Then Achiman appeared and said something to her in Hebrew that finally convinced her to let me go.

In July of 1974, the International Conference on High Energy Physics was held in London. I gave a talk in a parallel session[9] organized by Ben, that included talks by Nobelist T. D. Lee and future Nobelists Steve Weinberg and David Gross (who cited our work on the $\Delta I = \frac{1}{2}$ rule). I ran into an old friend from Brookhaven and Columbia, Mike Tannenbaum, who, upon seeing the session program, asked me: "What are you doing there with all the heavies?" One of the plenary session speakers on weak interactions was the theorist John Iliopoulos, who famously bet a case of wine that charm would be found within the year. He cited our papers on rare K decays and the $\Delta I = \frac{1}{2}$ rule, which were still in the preprint stage. The experimentalist Konrad Kleinknecht cited the K decay work, and also my 1971 paper on the decay of a strange "baryon" — the term for a hadron with half-integer spin — into a photon and a lighter baryon containing one less strange quark. My paper predicted the decay rate for one of these decays, giving a range of values that encompassed the result of a recent measurement. I remember his comment: "She did it all."

I had undertaken a study of these baryon decays using a theorem from a beautiful 1958 paper by Francis Low that relates a process with the emission of a low energy photon to the same process without the photon — a precursor to the similar (approximate) theorems of chiral symmetry, involving pion, rather than photon, emission. I also used the approximate flavor and chiral symmetries of the strong interactions. Theorists expected that the dominant

---

[9] Parallel sessions on specialized topics are run concurrently and attended by those most interested in a particular sub-field; plenary sessions summarize the work presented in parallel sessions and are attended by everyone at the conference.

contribution would be that obtained from Low's theorem. If this were the case, Low's theorem would have allowed a measurement of the probability for the first baryon to simply convert to the second one, which was of some interest to theorists at the time. I set out to do a calculation of this contribution for one of these decays that had already been observed. The evaluation of the decay probability was complicated, and I struggled with an early computer language, called Fortran, to do the calculation. In those days we had to type the program into a machine that punched holes in cards, which were then inserted into a very large computer that churned out the results on long sheets of paper. I was forever making typos that crashed my program. Eventually I enlisted the help of my friend Tini Veltman, who got the program running, but the answer kept coming out as a long string of zeros after the decimal point before a nonzero number appeared. Finally I understood that the probability I was trying to calculate was indeed exactly zero, because of the flavor and chiral symmetries of the theory. That lame attempt at a numerical calculation was my last. Since then I have relied on pencil and paper — and on my students and younger collaborators — when numerical work is indispensable.

By the end of the London conference I suddenly found myself elevated to a sort of star status. Even my old nemesis Bernard Gregory warmly greeted me as a friend and colleague (in French, much to Ben's surprise).

Our paper with Jon Rosner was distributed as a preprint in August of that year, with the caveat: "Our discussion is largely based on intuition gained from the familiar, but not necessarily understood, phenomenology of known hadrons, and predictions must be interpreted only as guidelines for experimenters." We also highlighted some hints of charm that had appeared in the experimental literature:

- In 1970, a group led by Leon Lederman had found an increase in the production rate of $\mu^+\mu^-$ pairs in proton collisions with nuclei when the dimuon mass was about three billion electron volts. This could be interpreted as the production of a spin-one charm–anticharm bound state (which we called ϕ_c, in analogy with the $s\bar{s}$ spin-one state called ϕ, or phi), which decays into a muon pair, if the mass of the charm quark is about 1.5 billion electron volts, as Ben and I had predicted. (Upon reading our paper, Leon called Ben to say that we were very gullible.)

- In 1971, the Japanese physicists Kiyoshi Niu, Eiko Mikumo and Yasuko Maeda were studying cosmic rays in emulsions. They found an event that appeared to be a particle with a mass of 1.78 billion electron volts decaying into a π^+ and a π^0; this could be a charm–antidown bound state (which we called D^+, after Bjorken and Glashow, who had first proposed charm in 1964).

- At the 1974 London conference, Carlo Rubbio reported that his group had found two events with a dimuon produced in neutrino collisions with nuclei. They could be interpreted as arising from an underlying two-step process. A ν_μ converts into a μ^- by colliding with a down quark, turning it into a charm quark that decays into a strange quark, a μ^+ and a ν_μ.

- Experiments at SLAC in 1973 and 1974 had found an unexpected rise with energy in the probability for e^+e^- annihilation into hadrons. The theoretical prediction for this process, including the leading QCD corrections, had been calculated in 1973 by Tom Appelquist and Howard Georgi. We compared the theoretical predictions with experiment for the cases with and without charm, and showed that the observation was consistent with theory if charmed particles were being produced at energies higher than three billion electron volts.

The year at Fermilab marked an important turning point in my career, which was perhaps enabled in part by the absence of the rather patronizing attitudes towards women that I had encountered in Europe. The civil rights struggles and consciousness-raising of the 1960s had at least led to a more thoughtful behavior on the part of white men, if not a great deal of progress for blacks or women, in terms of income levels and other indicators of parity. It's not that the issues of feminism and equality were nonexistent; rather they were a subject of lively debate. I can't remember the subject of a lunch conversation that prompted me to say (half in humor) something to the effect that liberal white men have no problem accepting black men as their equals, but they still have problems with women. In this context "white" included Asian — there was no shortage of Asian men in physics, but women were still very scarce, and blacks much scarcer yet. (Ben was well aware of what I meant; before I got past "liberal white men," he interjected to finish the sentence with "are male chauvinist pigs.")

With Val Telegdi and Bruno Zumino in Santa Barbara, 1993.

On another occasion we were having dinner with Jim and Barbara Vercoe and with Leon Lederman. We had become good friends with the Vercoes through their son Dave, who was Alain's classmate and best friend during our stay there. Jim was a physician, and Barbara was a full time mother of six. At some point Jean-Marc and Leon were consulting me about a theoretical issue. At the end of the conversation Jim asked me: "Did they answer your question?" to which Jean-Marc quickly replied: "She answered ours."

That year also led to a close friendship with Ben and his family, and I think his experience working with me subtly influenced his own attitudes. I had the impression that he came to regret the fact that Marianne had given up her medical studies when they married. He began to encourage her to return to school. She did embark on a career after Ben's death, and we stayed in touch for a very long time, visiting her during stays at Fermilab both before and after my move to the US with Bruno Zumino. I think the last time Bruno and I saw her was in 1988, when she came to Washington, D.C., for the E. O. Lawrence Award ceremony at the Department of Energy. We had lunch together in the House cafeteria and sat in on congressional deliberations for a while.

My last memory of that year at Fermilab is watching Richard Nixon's resignation speech, which earned Jean-Marc and myself a bottle of Chivas Regal, as payment on a bet with Peter Lyman.

CERN Again

Our family returned to CERN in the fall of 1974. I was suddenly very much in demand. I was appointed to a committee to discuss how CERN could step up its own search for charm. What I mostly remember about that committee is that Sergio Fubini, a former theory group leader and CERN elder statesman, was reading either Time or Newsweek throughout most of the discussion, and that the meetings were in a director's conference room on the top floor of a small tower, with no women's restroom.

I don't remember whether this was before or after the November revolution, sparked by the simultaneous announcement by teams at Brookhaven and SLAC of the discovery of a new particle that decayed into a charged lepton and its antiparticle. It was dubbed J at BNL (J looks like the Chinese character for "Ting," the name of the BNL group leader) and ψ (psi) at SLAC (the Greek letter ψ resembled the observed event shape), and known forever after as J/ψ. Its mass of about three billion electron volts confirmed that the bump in the production rate found earlier by the Lederman group was not just a statistical fluke. That discovery led to the Nobel Prize for the Brookhaven group leader Samuel Ting and for Burt Richter, who had been the force behind the electron–positron collider at SLAC — to the disgruntlement of Leon, who had yet to win a Nobel Prize for the discovery of the muon neutrino, and who had been the first to recognize the potential for discovery in the study of dilepton production in nucleon collisions, the production mechanism used at BNL. At the time of the November revolution, Leon was studying this process using the CERN proton–proton collider, and would call my office periodically to tell me that his group had ruled out a new spin-one particle with masses over a range of values just below and just above three billion electron volts. When I asked why they didn't look at three billion, the rather curious answer was something to the effect that there were "too many events" in that mass region.

However, the charm interpretation of the new particle was far from universally accepted at the time. There was a competing theory that posited that "colored" bound states of quarks should exist along with the known "colorless" states. For example the color carried by a red quark in a pion is canceled by that of its companion "anti-red" antiquark, and a proton made of a blue quark, a green quark and a red quark is "white" and has no net color. The idea was that the new particle might be made of, say, a red quark and an "anti-blue" antiquark. Probably there were other hypotheses that I no longer remember. The day after the announcement I was invited to Paris to lay out the implications of the discovery for both the color and charm hypotheses. John Ellis, at the time a junior staff scientist at CERN, and I were asked to debate with John Ward whether the newly found particle was a sign of manifest color or of charm. John Ellis and I probably won the debate (we were rooting for charm), but what I mostly remember was that Ward repeatedly referred to my paper with Ben and Jon Rosner as "Lee, Rosner and Gaillard," not in the normal alphabetical order that theoretical particle physicists use. (Once when Ben and I wrote a letter submitting one of our papers, the secretary who typed it put Ben's name first, much to Ben's consternation.)

Then came the long wait for "open charm," which means a bound state of a charmed particle and an uncharmed one (u, d or s); such states carry the charm quantum number, and, like strange particles, can be produced only in pairs (except in weak interactions, where a neutrino collision can convert a down quark to a charm quark, for example). The lightest charmed particle was expected to have a mass of about two billion electron volts. Already back at Fermilab Tom Ferbel — whom I knew as Tommy from my Brookhaven days — told us that charmed particles with masses up to about that value were already ruled out. My calculation with Ben had come up with a prediction of 1.5 billion electron volts for the charm quark mass, consistent with a J/ψ mass of about 3 billion electron volts, but the first version of our manuscript cited the value 2. My husband Jean-Marc read the manuscript very carefully, and said "You don't find 2, you find 1.5." So we corrected the paper to be more truthful, but also scrambled to raise the value of the mass, exploiting the uncertainties arising from the poor understanding of low energy strong interaction effects, and added an appendix that managed to get a charm quark mass of two billion electron volts, using an argument loosely based on color conservation. Our present better understanding of QCD shows that the argument in the appendix is too naive, and the original prediction was the right one. Even worse, the abstract[10] of our paper said only that we concluded that the charm quark must have a mass no larger than five billion electron volts, something that I had forgotten until many years later, when Michael Dine pointed out the discrepancy between our abstract and the value in the text during a workshop at Santa Barbara. When he asked me why, I just told him we were cowardly, since everyone was saying charm wasn't there at such a low mass. As time went on, after my return to CERN, I heard much of the same. Someone came up to me in the cafeteria and asked: "When are you going to stop believing in charm?" Jon Rosner reports that SLAC theorist Dick Blankenbecler remarked to him: "Don't give up the ship. It has just begun to sink."

And there was kaon counting. People like Tom Ferbel were looking for charm production in strong interactions. However if charmed particles had masses as low as two billion electron volts, they should have been produced in pairs at the SLAC electron–positron collider. Recall that down quarks decay to up quarks 20 times more often than strange quarks do, and that the GIM cancellation mechanism works if charm quarks decay to strange quarks 20 times more often than they decay to down quarks. So one would expect a lot of kaons to be produced when the total energy of the electron and positron exceeds four billion electron volts, allowing the production of two charmed particles. There were many blackboard sessions where I gave detailed arguments as to why the observed number of kaons was consistent with the production of charm (and one of the participants at these sessions wrote up my arguments in a paper). Adding to the confusion was the fact that we had underestimated the number of pions that would be produced, along with a kaon, in charm decay. (One reason for this is that we had used the wrong value for the

---

[10]A synopsis of the paper that appears at the beginning of the article.

parameter that determines the probability to emit an extra pion, due to two different conventions for its definition. Either I was never aware of this, or I had forgotten about it, until I was preparing a talk for Jon Rosner's retirement celebration in 2010 and I came across this embarrassing fact in Jon's own historical account of the search for charm written in 1999.)

One signature for charm that we had pointed out is an apparent violation of the so-called "$\Delta S = \Delta Q$ rule" of the Cabibbo theory. For example, a muon antineutrino $\bar{v}_\mu$ can convert an up quark u into a strange quark s by turning into a μ^+. The strange quark is assigned strangeness -1, and the up quark carries no strangeness, so the change ΔS in the strangeness of the quarks (and therefore of the hadrons observed in particle detectors) is -1. The quark electric charge Q changes from $\frac{2}{3}$ to $-\frac{1}{3}$, in agreement with the rule. One gets the neutrino-induced strangeness changing processes by replacing all four fermions with their antiparticles (v_μ, $\bar{u}$. $\bar{s}$, μ^-), which have the opposite signs of S and Q, so ΔS and ΔQ are now both $+1$.

However if charm is produced, there can be events when a v_l turns into an l^- by converting a down quark d to a charm quark, which then decays into s, u and $\bar{d}$, and the rule will appear to be violated. In March of 1975, a group at Brookhaven led by Bob Palmer and Nick Samios reported a bubble chamber event that could be interpreted as the production of a charmed baryon and a muon μ^- in the collision of a muon neutrino with a proton, and the subsequent decay of the charmed baryon into a Λ, three π^+ and one π^-, thus violating the $\Delta S = \Delta Q$ rule: the proton has $S = 0$, $Q = +1$, while the final state hadrons have $S = -1$, $Q = +2$, so strangeness is decreased by one unit, while the baryon electric charge *increases* by one unit. The $\Lambda + 4\pi$ state had a mass of 2462 million electron volts, in approximate agreement with a prediction made shortly before in a paper by Alvaro De Rujula, Howard Georgi and Shelly Glashow.

In July of 1975, I gave a series of lectures on weak interactions at a summer school in Cargèse, Corsica. The last lecture was on charmed particles. There was a young upstart graduate student, Serge Rudaz, from a group at Cornell that was busy calculating the properties of the higher mass states of "charmonium," a name that had been coined by Tom Appelquist and David Politzer to describe all the charm–anticharm bound states, in analogy with the name positronium for electron–positron bound states. Serge kept interrupting me to object that none of those states had been found. Probably as we were speaking, a group at the electron–positron collider DESY in Hamburg, Germany, announced the first observation of one of these states. The biannual Lepton–Photon conference was held at Stanford in August of that year, and Bjorn Wiik presented results from DESY. In his talk he announced the discovery of a state with the quantum numbers and expected mass of the particle Ben and I had named "η_c," since it is the charmonium counterpart of a bound state of light quarks, called η (eta), with the same quantum numbers. Ben and I were in attendance, waiting for Bjorn to proclaim the discovery of the η_c, but he declined to commit himself as to its identity and called it X, causing Ben to slap his hands on his knees in frustration. Unfortunately Ben did not live to see the particle become officially known as η_c.

However, "open charm" — bound states of a charmed and an uncharmed particle — had yet to be found. Finally, in June of 1976, I got a phone call from Ben who said: "Charm has been found." A group at SLAC led by Gerson Goldhaber and François Pierre had found evidence for the decay of a state with a mass of 1865 million electron volts that decayed into an electrically charged final state with a kaon and one or three pions. These were the anticipated mass and two of the anticipated final states of a $c\bar{d}$ bound state, called D^+, and its antiparticle.

The confusion in the search for charm at SLAC had been further compounded by the production of a new charged lepton, called τ (tau), with a mass very close to that of the D-meson — a situation reminiscent of the π-μ confusion in the earlier cosmic ray data due to the proximity of their masses. (The pion had been predicted by Hideki Yukawa as the mediator of the nuclear force; the muon was totally unexpected.) The τ was uncovered by a group led by Marty Perl that in 1975 reported the observation of electron–positron collisions which produced an electron and a muon in the final state, along with "missing energy"; that is, the energy of the two charged leptons did not add up to the total beam energy. These events could be interpreted as the production and decay of a pair of new leptons (τ^+, τ^-), with one τ decaying to an electron and two neutrinos, and the other to a muon and two neutrinos. It took about a year for the particle physics community to accept this interpretation, but any theorist who was paying attention realized immediately that the existence of a third charged lepton, with its accompanying third neutrino (which was later confirmed) implied a third pair of quarks in order to preserve the relation (see page 50) between quark and lepton electric charges which is needed to ensure that the theory is fully gauge invariant. So now the snapshot of elementary particles and forces had become

Force	Matter	Mediator	
strong	uuu, ddd, sss, ccu, bbb, ttt	$gggggggg$	
electroweak	above + e, μ, τ, ν_e, ν_μ, ν_τ	γ, $W^\pm$, Z	H
gravitational	all	h	

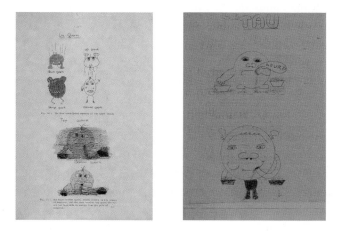

The quarks, from B. Gaillard and M. K. Gaillard, LAPP-TH-13 (1980) (left), and the heavy tau and the heavier W bossson, from B. Gaillard and F. Martin, CERN-TH-2803 (1980) (right).

The pair of new quarks (t, b) were initially called "truth" and "beauty" by some, but most of the community settled on the less pretentious names "top" and "bottom," first introduced by Haim Harari at the 1975 Stanford Lepton–Photon Symposium in analogy with up and down. They have the same electroweak quantum numbers as the pairs (u, d) and (c, s). Two years after the discovery of the τ, a group led by Leon Lederman at Fermilab found the lightest spin-1 $b\bar{b}$ bound state with a mass[11] of

---

[11] GeV is short for giga electron volts, that is, a billion electron volts.

9.5 GeV, which they called Υ (Upsilon) — following a false discovery ("oops, Leon") at a lower mass. The $W^\pm$ and Z were discovered in 1983 at the CERN proton–antiproton collider SPS, with masses of about 80 and 90 GeV, as had been predicted by the electroweak theory using neutrino scattering neutral current data. The top quark, with a mass of about 170 GeV, was not discovered until 1995, when a higher energy proton–antiproton collider, the Tevatron, was up and running at Fermilab. By that time very precise measurements of the Z mass at the high energy electron–positron collider LEP at CERN, and of the $W^\pm$ mass at the Tevatron, had allowed a prediction of the top quark mass. Just as the properties of kaons had allowed a prediction of the charm quark mass through its role in multiple interactions, similar effects in W and Z properties are sensitive to the t mass, as Tini Veltman had pointed out in 1977. The H in the table stands for the "Higgs particle," named after Sir Peter Higgs, who proposed it. The 2014 film *Particle Fever*, perhaps more aptly, depicts the Higgs at the center of the particle panoply, surrounded by gauge bosons and then by matter. Not only is it needed to explain why, unlike the photon γ and the gluons g, the W and Z have masses, although the full electroweak theory has an exact gauge invariance; it is also needed to give masses to fermions, and therefore to everything. It is often called the "God particle" in the popular press, because without it there would be no galaxies or people in the universe. A book by Lederman (Dell Publishing, 1993) had this expression as its title because, according to Leon, his editors would not let him use "The Goddamn Particle," which presumably reflected the extreme difficulty in detecting it. Indeed it was not until July 4, 2012, that the observation of a "Higgs-like" particle was announced by groups working with the ATLAS and CMS detectors at the very high energy proton–proton CERN collider LHC (Large Hadron Collider), part of which lies under the house in Echenevex where I had lived. The Higgs particle weighed in at about 125 GeV, and its discovery completed the picture of what had become known as the Standard Model of particle physics.

Once charm was confirmed, I was asked to speak about charm and related issues at many conferences, including the annual neutrino conference. A group led by Carlo Rubbio had found something called the "high-y anomaly" in neutrino interactions with nuclei, which simply meant that there were a larger number of events than the theory predicted for a particular range of energies of the leptons in the final state. In fact, the onset of charm production predicted such an excess, but a much smaller one. At one of these conferences Carlo complained: "Why don't you believe us? It's what you predicted." Eventually the high-y anomaly disappeared, and eventually Carlo won the Nobel Prize for the discovery of the W and Z particles, but that was far from my last encounter with him. It was also at one of these conferences, when I was chatting with experimental colleagues, that my old friend Jack Steinberger, who had led beautifully precise neutrino experiments, but was never involved in the search for charm, remarked somewhat ruefully "the high priests of charm."

Two Weeks in the Soviet Union

In June of 1977, the neutrino conference was held near Tblisi, in the Baksan Valley of the Caucasus mountains of Georgia. I had also been invited to spend the week before the conference in Moscow, at the Institute for Theoretical and Experimental Physics (ITEP). My friend Alexander (Sacha) Dolgov was supposed to pick me up at the Moscow airport, but there was no sign of him when I arrived. I sat in the airport for an hour or two, wondering how I would survive in a city where I didn't know the language and had no idea where I was supposed to go. Finally Sacha appeared; apparently he had gotten the time of my arrival wrong. He drove me to an ITEP apartment house where I found a nice room, closed off by French doors from the rest of the apartment, where two male Italian physicists were staying, although there was no sign of them when I arrived. I woke up hungry the next morning, and boiled an egg that I found in the refrigerator. As it turned out, we were supposed to buy our own food, and I later encountered an irate Italian who was the owner of the egg. Then the powers that be decided it was improper for me to share an apartment with two men, and they moved me to a shared room with a friend and colleague Glennys Farrar. Having to give up my privacy was compensated for by the fact that Glennys had already been in Moscow for a week or so and was able to show me where to shop for food. I had not anticipated the incredibly long lines, and made the mistake of buying an ice cream cone before getting in line for groceries — including a replacement for the stolen egg — and I didn't notice my dripping ice cream until someone tapped me on the shoulder.

There was a complicated arrangement for paying my expenses, since different European organizations had agreements with different Soviet laboratories. Although I was physically at CERN, where there was an exchange agreement with ITEP, I worked for the French CNRS. As a consequence I had to give a talk at the Institute for High Energy Physics (IHEP) in Serpukhov, about 60 miles south of Moscow. I was also expected to give a theory talk at ITEP. Since I knew that talks among Russian theorists could last for hours, in order to extricate myself from endless questions, I scheduled my talk for the morning of the same day, starting an hour or so before I would be picked up by a driver from IHEP. Besides the driver there was the requisite "interpreter," chatting endlessly during the drive. My host at IHEP was Semen Gershtein, who earlier had come to my office at CERN with a small Russian doll to personally invite me to speak at the Tblisi neutrino conference. Bearing gifts was standard for Soviets visiting the West; we reciprocated, usually with books, from Agatha Christie to politics. My last trip to the Soviet Union, in the late 1980s, was for a conference in the mountains near Yerevan, Armenia, where I left a tape of Bob Dylan songs that my friends had put together for me. Once we were able to leave — the Yerevan airport had been closed because of a protest related to the Armenian conflict with Azerbaijan — my by-then husband Bruno Zumino and I went to Moscow. I was reading Gorbachev's "Perestroika," which my son Alain had given me; it had not yet appeared in the Soviet Union, so it stayed with friends in Moscow.

As soon as I entered the main IHEP building, there was some commotion, and I was told I had to go to the ladies' room to brush my hair. Slightly bewildered, I was escorted to lunch, after which I gave my talk, and then Gershtein gave me an extended tour of the laboratory. When the tour was over he took me to a car with no interpreter, handed me a note, and crossed the street. The note was a telegram announcing the death of Ben Lee. I looked across the street and saw Semen Gershtein crying. I wondered how he had — so very thoughtfully — managed to avoid the interpreter.

Back in Moscow I would have liked to have been alone longer, and regretted the loss of my single room. Ben had originally been scheduled to speak at the Tblisi conference, but had to cancel because of Fermlab's annual Program Advisory Committee (PAC — later "Program" was replaced by "Physics") in Aspen, Colorado. He was killed when a truck crossed the highway divider and turned over onto the car in which he was driving his family to their Aspen condo. I soon got word from Jean-Marc that Ben's wife Marianne had told him not to cancel the visit to the Lee family that our children Alain and Dominique had planned that summer. They were the same ages as Jeff and Irene Lee and had become good friends with them during our stay at Fermilab. I remember some sort of competitive game they played in the pool with the sisters perched on their brothers' shoulders.

There was a strong overlap between my work and that of the younger ITEP theorists, among them Mikhail (Misha) Shifman and Valentin Zakharov. We had many long blackboard sessions, including the previously eluded discussion of the topic of my talk, a paper I had written with Mike Chanowitz, who was visiting CERN from Lawrence Berkeley Laboratory (LBL), and John Ellis. In early 1974, Howard Georgi and Shelly Glashow had proposed a simple and elegant model that unified the electroweak and the strong interactions — just as the GWS theory had unified the weak and electromagnetic interactions. Then alternative models for this further unification, collectively known as Grand Unified Theories (or GUTs, as we dubbed them) were proposed. Mike, John and I had studied constraints on these theories, based both on assuring the mathematical consistency of the theory and avoiding conflict with experiment. At the end of our prolonged discussion, Misha said: "Now we know how to build a unified theory." Valentin invited Glennys and me to dinner one evening, along with some of our Russian colleagues. Valentin, who never met Ben personally, said that he had tried to add a dedication to Ben in a paper of his that was being published in *Physical Review Letters*, but was refused. (I had the same problem years later when one of my former students at Berkeley died suddenly.) Fortunately, John, Dimitri Nanopoulos, Serge Rudaz (who by then had become a friend and collaborator) and I were able to dedicate our next paper to Ben, since *Nuclear Physics*, the European journal of choice by then, had no such policy — or almost no such policy. In 1981, Bruno Zumino and I wanted to dedicate a paper to Andrei Sakharov, still under house arrest, on the occasion of his 60th birthday. The journal editors refused, presumably for fear of jeopardizing their agreements with the Soviet Union. We finally prevailed, with the proviso that we add a strictly scientific reason for the dedication.

I also had friends among ITEP experimentalists who were involved in an experiment at CERN. One of them arranged a day-time flight to Tblisi for me. There were a handful of passengers, all Westerners, who were seated directly over the wings, so we couldn't see much of what was below us.

I arrived at the conference still in a state of shock and sadness. My ITEP host Lev Okun did his best to cheer me up, and I met Soviet physicists from other laboratories, including our "competitors" Khriplovich and Vainshtein from Novosibirsk, Siberia. But there were also many Western scientists, and I was struck by the stark difference in sensitivity. One of my French colleagues called out to me and asked me if I had heard that Lee had died, as though it was a piece of news that might be of mild interest to me. I closed my talk with a few words about Ben, to the surprise of the West German session chair to whom it hadn't occurred that we might have been close friends. Possibly because of their more difficult living — and working — conditions, the Soviets placed more value on human relations than did their Western counterparts.

For the flight back to Moscow, we were strictly under the control of the Soviet travel agency Intourist, and the foreigners were forced to fly in the middle of the night. In the evening when we were waiting for departure

Lecturing on neutrino-induced production of charm at Tblisi.

time, Lev Okun invited me to his room to talk with him and Vladimir Gribov, from the Ioffe Institute in Leningrad, whom I had not met before the conference. Gribov's work on strong interactions was widely known in the West, but, if I remember correctly, he had not yet been permitted to travel outside the Soviet Union. They must have been sure that the room was safe, because more often conversations of this sort between Soviets and Westerners took place on long walks, out of earshot from other people. (During the Soviet era, every international conference had two or three "delegates" — always the same faces — who never spoke but just wandered around listening to conversations; we referred to them as the KGB guys.) We spoke of many things, including politics. I was a bit embarrassed when Lev mentioned Jimmy Carter's book, which he had read and I had not. Then suddenly Glennys appeared at the door and the conversation abruptly ended; somehow the mood was broken. Since it was still not time for us to leave, Glennys and I joined a party in the room of Henry Lubatti, so by the time we boarded the plane I had drunk enough to make the trip bearable.

When it was time for me to leave Moscow, Sacha Dolgov took me to the airport where he told me I could not take any Soviet money out of the country. So I dumped my remaining rubles and kopecks into a collection box, with the comment that I was contributing to the economy of the Soviet Union, and we proceeded to the check-in counter. There I was informed that my Aeroflot seat was not available, and that I could not board the plane. This was followed by a lengthy conversation in Russian between Sacha and the woman behind the counter, after which I was issued a first-class ticket, and had a very pleasant journey home.

Not long after my return to CERN from Fermilab, John Ellis had approached me with a suggestion about how to treat the decays of charmed particles into uncharmed hadrons. In my paper with Ben and Jon Rosner, we had assumed that the enhancement that Ben and I had found for the weak interactions of two quarks in an antisymmetric combination could be carried over to the decays of charmed particles. John pointed out that the QCD corrections should be less important in charm decays because the effective energy scale $m_c c^2$, set by the mass m_c of the charm quark, was higher than that for ordinary hadrons, and therefore, due to asymptotic freedom, the QCD effects were weaker. He convinced me, and with Dimitri Nanopoulos, then a CERN Fellow, we wrote a paper arguing that all the effects that contribute to the predominance of strange particle decays with $\Delta I = \frac{1}{2}$ are less efficient in charm decays. When Ben read our paper, he at first objected, but I eventually won him over. That was the beginning of a six-year collaboration at CERN with John and others, most often with Dimitri. Our second paper dealt with the Higgs particle.

The Higgs Particle

In addition to the W and Z particles that had yet to be detected because their predicted masses were beyond the reach of existing accelerator and collider facilities, the electroweak theory required a scalar particle, the Higgs particle H, with an unknown mass; that is, the theory did not predict its mass, but simply related it to another unknown parameter. As mentioned before, the Higgs particle is necessary to explain why the $W^{\pm}$ and Z are massive, unlike the photon, and indeed why these particles are even distinguishable from one another. Both the electroweak theory and QCD are invariant under gauge transformations that turn one type of particle into another.

In QCD, gluons carrying different color charges transform into one another, as do quarks of different color but the same flavor: a red up quark can turn into a blue up quark without changing the laws of physics, provided the other quarks and gluons transform accordingly. As a consequence, we cannot perform any experiment that determines the colors of the quarks and gluons that are produced in a particle interaction.

The gauge transformations of the electroweak theory change particles of the same color but different flavor into one another. If the electroweak gauge symmetry were respected in nature, we would not be able to distinguish a W^+ from a W^- or an electron from its neutrino. We know that the laws of physics must be invariant for the theory to be well-defined. If the symmetry were not respected, the predictions of the theory would break down at higher orders in the couplings, but by now experiments have verified that the predicted multi-interaction contributions are correct to a very high precision. Therefore we must conclude that the laws of physics are invariant, but that the state of nature that we live in does not respect the symmetry of these laws. This situation is known as "spontaneous" symmetry breaking.

Spontaneous Symmetry Breaking

- The laws of physics are invariant under rotations in space. Therefore a bunch of electrons in empty space will have spins pointing in random directions, and if the group of electrons is rotated around any spatial axis, it will be indistinguishable from the unrotated group: the spherical symmetry of the laws of nature remains unbroken. However, for electrons in a ferromagnet, the preferred state — the state of lowest energy — is with all the electron spins aligned; they all want to point in the same direction. It doesn't matter what direction they point in, but once they are aligned in some direction the system is no longer invariant under rotations.

- Imagine that the earth is a perfect sphere. An ant crawling on the surface of the earth has no way to determine where it is. Now turn on the earth's magnetic field and give the ant a compass. It can now distinguish north from south, but not east from west. The magnetic field breaks the earth's spherical symmetry to a cylindrical symmetry.

- Drop an olive into a cylindrical wine glass that is rounded at the bottom. The olive will settle at the bottom in the center of the glass: the cylindrical symmetry of the system (wine glass plus olive) remains unbroken. A better idea is to drop the olive into a cylindrical martini glass. If this glass has a small cylindrical bump at the bottom, the symmetry is preserved only if the olive lands on the top of the bump, an unlikely and unstable situation. Eventually the olive will settle somewhere in the valley surrounding the bump, thereby spontaneously breaking the cylindrical symmetry of the system.

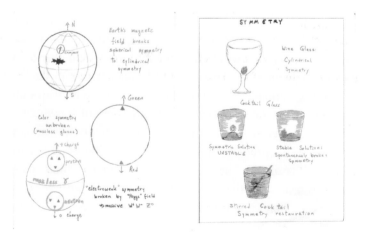

Spontaneous breaking of the electroweak gauge symmetry can be understood if a field — known as the Higgs field — permeates all space and time, just as the presence of an electromagnetic field breaks rotational symmetry. And, just as the photon is a quantized bit of electromagnet field, there must be a Higgs particle, that is, a quantized bit of Higgs field.

The electromagnetic field has two distinct components — electric and magnetic fields — with two associated particles: left-spinning and right-spinning photons. The Higgs field is invariant under rotations, so it preserves rotational symmetry, but it is not invariant under the electroweak gauge symmetry. It has *four* distinct components, corresponding to four spin-zero particles: H^+, H^0 and their antiparticles $\bar{H}^0$, H^-. The $\bar{H}^0$ and H^- transform into one another in the same way as left-spinning neutrinos and electrons transform into each other, and H^+, H^0 transform in the same way as right-spinning e^+, $\bar{\nu}_e$. The energy of empty space depends on the sum of the strengths of the four Higgs components; it does not matter how these strengths are distributed among the four components. One can think of the components as forming a vector that points toward the surface of a sphere in an abstract, mathematical space, with, for example, the proton sitting on the North Pole, and the neutron at the South Pole. If the Higgs field points north to south or south to north, the proton becomes distinguishable from the neutron, but there is one set of transformations — a trip due east or west on the sphere — that leaves flavor unchanged and remains a symmetry of nature. This unbroken symmetry is identified with the gauge symmetry of QED.

The energy contained in the Higgs field resembles the gravitational pull on the olive in the martini glass. The vertical direction represents the energy, the radial horizontal direction outward from the center of the glass represents the value v of the Higgs field (the square root of the total field strength), and the horizontal direction around the valley at the bottom of the glass represents the direction in which the field is pointing in the abstract space. The point in the valley where the field sits doesn't matter, just as the olive can fall anywhere in the valley at the bottom of the martini glass. But, like the olive, once the Higgs field settles into a fixed position in the valley — in this case a fixed orientation in the abstract space — the electroweak symmetry is broken.

When a beam of light, which is really a beam of photons, travels through a medium such as water, it interacts with the electrons in the medium, which makes it travel more slowly than the speed of light c as seen by an outside observer, who cannot see it bouncing around at its usual speed c from electron to electron; this could be interpreted as the photons acquiring a mass in the medium. In the same way, particles that interact with the Higgs field are slowed down, like a bug sloshing through molasses, and acquire a mass. Since this field covers all space for all time (except during the first few milliseconds after the Big Bang: symmetry is restored at very high temperatures, as in the stirred cocktail) we simply say the particles that interact with the Higgs field have masses.

The Higgs particle, which corresponds to a small fluctuation of the Higgs field away from its preferred value v, also interacts with its own field, and therefore also acquires a mass. Specifically, a vertical fluctuation in the martini glass costs energy; a fluctuation in this direction has a mass determined by the steepness of the slope near the bottom of the glass. It is this massive scalar particle that is identified with "the" Higgs particle. On the other hand, very small fluctuations along the valley, that is, fluctuations away from the chosen *orientation* of the field, cost no energy, so the corresponding particles are massless.

Now here is a paradox. The spin-1 gauge fields and fermions of the electroweak theory would be massless if the symmetry were exact. A massless gauge particle, like the photon, has just two possible spin orientations: left- or right-spinning along its direction of motion. Since, as explained before, a massless particle, always traveling at the speed of light c, can never be brought to rest, its spin orientation along its axis of motion is fixed in the absence of interactions. However a massive particle *can* be brought to rest, and once at rest its spin can be made to point in any direction. But for a spin-1 particle at rest there are three possible spin orientations (e.g., up, north and east) which are equally possible. So by sloshing through the Higgs molasses, the Ws and Z acquire not only a mass, but an extra spin component. Where does it come from? It comes from the three extra spinless Higgs bosons; they have no component of spin along the axis of motion of the Ws and Z. These three extra spinless particles are said to be "eaten" by the Ws and Z; they do not appear as separate particles in nature.

Apparently prompted by Dimitri, John asked me if I would be interested in doing a comprehensive study of the properties of the Higgs boson, similar in spirit to the GLR analysis of charmed particles. I agreed, and we embarked on a systematic study of mechanisms for Higgs production and for its decays.

The mass of an elementary fermion f is equal to the Higgs field value v multiplied by the constant g_f whose square determines the strength of its coupling to the Higgs field, and the mass of a vector boson V is equal to $v/\sqrt{2}$ times its coupling g_V to the Higgs field. The coupling g_f varies from fermion to fermion. However the constant g_w that determines the probability for turning a charged Higgs particle into an uncharged one via $W^{\pm}$ emission is the same as for that for turning an up quark into a down quark or an electron into a neutrino and so on. As a consequence, the value v of the Higgs field has actually been known since well before either the Higgs field or the GWS theory were even dreamt of. Radioactive nuclear decays occur when, say, a down quark converts to an up quark by emitting a W^- that itself converts to an electron and its antineutrino. The probability for each of these conversions is proportional to the square of g_w, and the probability for the overall process is determined by the ratio g_w/m_w, which is the same as $\sqrt{2}/v$ because $vg_w/\sqrt{2}$ is the mass m_w of the $W^{\pm}$; it appears in the denominator because the Heisenberg uncertainty principle limits the range $r = \hbar/m_w c$ of the interaction as discussed on page 42. In other words, the probability for a nuclear decay directly determines the Higgs field value v, with no high energy experiment required! Once we know v we know the coupling to the Higgs particle for any other particle whose mass is known: $g_f = m_f/v$ for fermions, and $g_V = \sqrt{2}\, m_V/v$ for vector bosons.

As a consequence, we were able to predict in detail Higgs production and decay rates — for a given Higgs mass. The caveat was that we had no clue as to the mass of the Higgs particle, except for a very weak lower bound. The reason was that the Higgs mass is proportional to the constant g_h that governs the strength of its coupling to itself, for which there were no data in the absence of its observation. We displayed our predictions for masses ranging from one million to 100 billion electron volts (just short of the 125 billion electron volt mass of the particle discovered at CERN in 2012), and ended our paper with an "apology" (much to Dimitri's chagrin) that we couldn't do better. Nevertheless, as the first comprehensive study of the properties of the Higgs particle, our paper had considerable impact. Our predictions evolved in time and were refined by others as the third family of fermions (τ, b, t) became established and their masses known — not until 1995 for the top quark. The failure to find the Higgs particle at the CERN electron–positron collider LEP set its mass at larger than 115 billion electron volts. The Tevatron at Fermilab, as it turns out, was within reach of discovering the Higgs particle, but was shut down for programmatic reasons before it could gather enough data at a sufficiently high energy to establish its existence. However an analysis of the data already taken was able to reveal a hint of the Higgs particle with a mass of about 125 billion electron volts, in agreement with the much higher precision data announced by the ATLAS and CMS experiments at the CERN LHC on July 4, 2012. The following year the Nobel Prize was awarded to François Englert who, together with the late Robert Brout, was the first to introduce what is now called the Higgs field, and to Peter Higgs, who first pointed out that there would necessarily be a particle associated with that field, the Higgs particle.

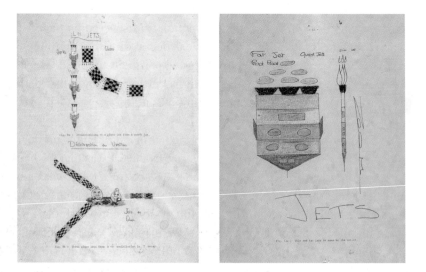

Jet images from B. Gaillard and M. K. Gaillard, LAPP-TH-13 (1980).

Gluon Jets

My subsequent papers with John and others at CERN covered a variety of topics in weak and strong interactions and beyond, including the interface of particle physics with cosmology. One notable contribution was a paper John and I wrote with Graham Ross. In 1975, an analysis of electron–positron annihilation into hadrons, led by Gail Hansen at SLAC, showed that the hadrons emerged as two collimated, back-to-back jets, with the same behavior as the back-to-back muons emitted in e^+e^- annihilation into $\mu^+\mu^-$. The SLAC result beautifully confirmed the hypothesis that the underlying process for annihilation into hadrons was in fact e^+e^- annihilation into $q\bar{q}$ by the same mechanism (photon exchange) as for muons, with the quarks, like the muons, having a half unit of spin. These results were confirmed with greater precision in subsequent collider experiments at higher energies, where the jets become more highly collimated. However sometimes a photon can appear in the final state, along with the muons or the quarks. The photon can be emitted from any fermion in the initial or final state. In the same way, since quarks couple to gluons, sometimes

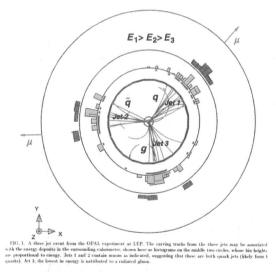

FIG. 1. A three jet event from the OPAL experiment at LEP. The curving tracks from the three jets may be associated with the energy deposits in the surrounding calorimeter, shown here as histograms on the middle two circles, whose bin heights are proportional to energy. Jets 1 and 2 contain muons as indicated, suggesting that these are both quark jets (likely from b quarks). Jet 3, the lowest in energy is attributed to a radiated gluon.

A jet image from Mary K. Gaillard, Paul D. Grannis, Frank J. Sciulli, *Rev. Mod. Phys.* 71 (1999) S96–S111.

a gluon g should accompany the quark pair, with the gluon emitted from one of the final state quarks. In fact this should occur more often than photon emission because the QCD coupling is stronger than the QED coupling. This means that there should be three jets some of the time, in which case the quark jets would not be back-to-back; instead there would be three jets lying in a plane. We determined the configurations of the final state hadrons for the case with no gluons, and including spinless gluons and gluons with one unit of spin. Three years after our paper was published, three-jet events were clearly established and the spin-one property of the gluon was confirmed. The 1995 High Energy and Particle Physics Prize of the European Physical Society was awarded to Paul Söding, Bjorn Wiik, Günter Wolf and Sau Lan Wu, the leaders of the TASSO experiment at PETRA, which was the first to observe three-jet events.

After we finished the three-jet paper, John went off somewhere for a month or two, and Alvaro De Rujula asked me if I would be interested in working with him on studying event patterns in electron–positron annihilation into hadrons, as a way of analyzing three-jet events in more detail. John joined us when he returned, and we were also joined by Emmanuel Floratos, a CERN Fellow from Greece, so our paper became known as the "alphabetical paper" (DEFG). We came up with a helpful yardstick that measured the amount of energy in the most energetic jet. John proposed calling this parameter "thrust," and thrust it became. We were apparently unaware — and I was unaware until a few years ago — that the previous year a paper proposing a very similar parameter, also called thrust, had been published by an MIT graduate student, Eddie Fahri. Writing up our results was something of a struggle because there was a rather unfriendly rivalry between John and Alvaro. Alvaro wrote the first draft, which John rewrote completely in a form unacceptable to Alvaro. So finally I came up with a compromise draft that essentially became the paper.

Bottom Quarks, Penguins and GUTS

In 1976, John, Dimitri and I had become aware that Sandip Pakvasa and Hirotaka Sugawara, and, independently, Luciano Maiani, had rediscovered the (until then essentially unknown in the West)

Kobayashi–Maskawa observation that the presence of a third quark pair (top, bottom) allowed for the possibility of *CP* violation in the electroweak theory. The existence of this third quark pair was now imposed by the apparent discovery of a third charged lepton (tau), in order to maintain the correct relation among fermion electric charges (see page 50). We wrote a paper somewhat provocatively entitled "Left-Handed Currents and *CP* Violation" — provocative because the "high-*y*" controversy, which Carlo Rubbia and I had argued about, was still around. The reported effect could be explained if there was a weak coupling of right-spinning light quarks *u*, *d* to right-spinning heavier quarks. Specifically, Michael Barnett showed that a right-right *u*-*b* coupling, with a *b* quark mass of about five billion electron volts, could fit the data. As it turned out, the excess of high-*y* events eventually disappeared, and the prediction of only left–left charged currents was verified. Nevertheless, when evidence for a new particle with a mass of about five billion electron volts began to surface it was widely assumed to be the *b* quark, although there was no information as to its electric charge, and it was *not* widely known that Mike Chanowitz, John and I had just predicted a *b* quark mass of about five billion electron volts for an entirely different reason.

The paper with Mike and John that I had discussed at ITEP during the week before the Tblisi neutrino meeting showed that the "minimal" version of the Georgi–Glashow GUT theory (the version that most easily avoided conflict with experiments) predicted a bottom to tau mass ratio in the range

$$m_b/m_\tau = 2 \text{ to } 5,$$

which, since the tau weighed about two billion electron volts, implied a bottom quark mass between four and ten billion electron volts. But, just as Ben and I had been too cowardly to pin down the charm quark mass in the abstract of our paper, the abstract of the preprint for this paper, which appeared in May of 1977, was considerably more vague. We were correcting the proofs for the published version of the paper in July, at around the same time I went to pick up Leon Lederman at the Geneva airport, and, through a screen near the baggage claim gate, he handed me a beautiful histogram showing clear evidence for a $b\bar{b}$ spin-one bound state–named Υ (Upsilon) by its discoverers — with a mass of about 10 billion electron volts, in other words, evidence for a bottom quark with a mass of about five billion electron volts. John quickly penciled in a correction to the abstract with our more precise prediction, but his handwriting was so bad that "to" was read as "60", and our prediction came out in print as

$$m_b/m_\tau = 2605,$$

implying a b-quark mass of over 5000 billion electron volts — and totally inaccessible to experiments at the time. This mass range is not even within reach of the LHC.

Around the same time as Leon's arrival in Geneva, the preprint of a paper appeared, by John, Dimitri, Serge Rudaz and myself, that had been prompted by the Upsilon discovery. This was the paper that we dedicated to Ben:

> *To our friend Benjamin W. Lee who cannot share with us the joys of new discoveries.*

It was also the paper that introduced the term "penguin" into the particle physics lexicon. We were studying the properties of B-mesons (bound states of a b or $\bar{b}$ and a light quark), including their weak decays into lighter hadrons. We considered contributions from the mechanism that had been proposed by Shifman, Vainshtein and Zakharov (SVZ) as an important contribution to the $\Delta I = \frac{1}{2}$ rule observed in strange particle decays. One evening, John went to a pub with Serge and Melissa Franklin, then a Stanford graduate student (and now a Harvard professor). Melissa and John started a game of darts, with Melissa imposing the stipulation that if John lost he had to use the word "penguin" in his next paper. Melissa didn't stay to finish the game, so Serge replaced her and beat John. John interpreted the result as a moral obligation to fulfill Melissa's condition. After some struggling with the problem, upon stopping by CERN after a party and under the influence of an "illegal substance," John realized that the diagrammatic representation of the SVZ mechanism resembled — or could be contorted so as to resemble — the shape of a penguin; hence it became a "penguin diagram." Since the literature was already replete with terms like "seagull diagram" and "tadpole diagram," no one questioned the terminology. Melissa's challenge to John earned her an acknowledgment in our paper, along with several eminent colleagues of ours and my then nine-year-old son, Bruno.

At the time that we were working on this paper, Bruno was attending a private school in Geneva, and came to CERN by bus after school. Our older children, Alain and Dominique, had attended elementary school in the nearby town of Gex in order to avoid the one-room Echenevex school with a single teacher who had a poor reputation. When we returned from Fermilab, they both entered the *Lycée Internationale* that had recently been established in Ferney-Voltaire, but the Gex elementary school no longer accepted students from Echenevex. So we looked for a private school for Bruno. Jean-Marc wanted to get him re-immersed in French; the only option was a Catholic school. After his first day there Bruno insisted on doing his catechism before his other homework. That enthusiasm wore off very quickly, but the school did not work out well.

From Wikipedia, the free encyclopedia

So the following year we put him in an English school in Geneva, with just one French class. Jean-Marc usually drove him to school in the morning, and he took the bus to CERN where he stayed an hour or so until I was ready to go home. Once I found him cowering in a corner of my office. When I pressed him to tell me what was wrong, he shamefacedly pulled out a small paper he had hidden between some books. It turned out that I had mistakenly bought him bus tickets at a lower fare than he was entitled to, and he had received a citation with a fine. Anyway Serge took advantage of Bruno's presence to have him check the result of a numerical integration by counting the squares under a graph of the integrand. The school problem was solved the following year when a very good international elementary school opened in Prevessin, near Ferney, and he, like his older siblings at the *Lycée*, was accepted because of his dual nationality.

This was not Bruno's only foray into particle physics. When he was 12, and about to enter the Ferney *Lycée*, the school went on strike, so I took him with me to a two-week school in Rabat, Morocco, where I was scheduled to lecture. The only other person accompanying a lecturer was the wife of my Orsay colleague Michel Gourdin. The first day of the school, my handsome young son with then-fashionable long blond hair and the comely Mme. Gourdin set out to take a tour of the city. They quickly acquired a retinue of Moroccan men, and were so traumatized that Mme. Gourdin stayed in her hotel room for the duration of the school, and Bruno came to the lectures with me. He kept himself entertained by drawing illustrations of the concepts in the lectures, some of which appear in these pages. My colleague François Martin, with whom Bruno had become good friends, and I used his drawings to illustrate the written versions of our lectures on QCD.

Shortly after Georgi and Glashow had proposed their GUT model, Georgi, Helen Quinn and Steve Weinberg showed that any model which unifies the strong and electroweak interactions into a single gauge theory, which is characterized by just one number — the "coupling constant" g that determines the common strength of these interactions at some energy scale — makes a prediction for the measurable parameters of the Standard Model.

The electroweak theory is characterized by two coupling constants. One is g_w for the couplings of W^+, W^- and W^0; the W^0 is an admixture of Z and the photon γ. Together the W^+, W^- and W^0 form the three components of a vector in the abstract space of rotations under the electroweak gauge transformations. The other admixture, called B, is a scalar in the abstract space and is the mediator of an Abelian gauge theory, with a different coupling constant g_b. The Higgs field changes under both sets of electroweak transformations, but one combination of W^0 and B, namely the photon γ, does not couple to the electrically neutral Higgs field and therefore remains massless when that field acquires a non-vanishing value. Imposing the correct QED couplings for the photon γ fixes the B couplings to fermions and to the Higgs field, except for the value of g_b. Both g_b and g_w are proportional to the electric charge e of the positron, with their values determined by the "weak mixing angle" $θ_w$, so-called because it specifies the admixture of B and W^0 within the photon. The other admixture of B and W^0 is the Z; measurement of the Z couplings in neutral current interactions fixed the remaining parameter $θ_w$ (and tested the consistency of the theory!).

The idea of grand unification is that there is a symmetry larger than those of QCD and the electroweak theory, and that encompasses them both. This symmetry is broken by the very large value V (much, much larger than the value v of the Higgs field of the Standard Model) of another Higgs field, that has no couplings to Standard Model gauge bosons, but gives large masses to the other gauge bosons associated with the larger gauge symmetry. At energies much larger than V this symmetry breaking is unimportant, and the coupling constants of the Standard Model gauge bosons should all be the same. Below that scale, higher order effects involving heavy states with masses of order V become negligible, while those involving lighter particles are still in play. As a consequence the three coupling constants of QCD and the electroweak theory evolve differently: the information that they are part of a single theory is lost. The strong coupling g_s grows as the energy decreases, the weak coupling g_w also grows but less quickly, and g_b, the coupling for the Abelian gauge theory (see box above), gets smaller at lower energies.

What Georgi, Quinn and Weinberg (GQW) did was to study how the couplings evolve from low energy to high. There are five parameters involved in the analysis: the three couplings g_s, g_w and g_b that are measured at low energy, the value V of the energy at which they become equal, and the common value g of the couplings at that energy. Requiring the three Standard Model couplings to equal g at the energy V amounts to three conditions on these five parameters.

Two of these conditions determine the values of V and g in terms of g_s, g_w and g_b — or in terms of g_s, e and θ_w, since g_w and g_b can be written in terms of e and θ_w. The third condition imposes a constraint relating the three measured parameters. GQW used the (very precisely) measured value of e and the (much less precisely) measured value of g_s to determine θ_w. They found a value for $\sin^2 \theta$ of about 0.17, considerably lower than experimenters had found at the time that John, Dimitri, Andrzej Buras and I began studying the Georgi–Glashow theory in detail. In fact initial results had given $\sin^2 \theta$ around 3/8, a value that, by a similar analysis, would have implied that g_w and g_b are the same at the scale of electroweak symmetry breaking (the Z mass) as Cecilia Jarlskog had been the first to point out.

By the time our paper (BEGN, dubbed "Begin," as in Menachem, by our colleagues — a 1980 paper on proton decay, with Buras replaced by Rudaz, was called "Reagan", as in Ronald, even though the correct acronym was EGNR) appeared in 1978, the experimental value of $\sin^2 \theta_w$ was between 0.22 and 0.26. Including additional contributions to the coupling constant evolution, we got a theoretical value of about 0.20. Later further refinements of the calculation and an improved determination of the strong coupling constant pushed this up to 0.21, and for a long time the uncertainties on both the measured and calculated numbers were large enough that there was apparent agreement between theory and experiment. However in 1991, shortly before I was asked to give the introductory lecture at the by then annual conference on superstring theory, an experimental group at CERN announced a value of about 0.23 with an error so small that it could not be reconciled with the theory. However, it *could* be reconciled with a version of grand unification involving a new symmetry, called supersymmetry, which entailed doubling the number of elementary particles. This was the first real hint of physics beyond the

> *Because it unifies QCD with the electroweak theory, the enlarged symmetry of the Georgi–Glashow theory includes transformations that turn quarks into antiquarks or into leptons, and the associated gauge bosons carry both color and electroweak charges. Like left-spinning up and down quarks and their right-spinning antiparticles, they form two color triplets, X and Y, and their antiparticles, which transform into one another under rotations in the abstract electroweak space. As a result they can mediate proton decays into, for example, a positron and a π^0 or an electron antineutrino and a π^+.*

Standard Model,[12] and it gave me something interesting to talk about: the implications of the result for superstring theory.

The main focus of BEGN was to refine the calculation of the bottom quark mass — we were able to narrow it down to the range 4.8–5.3 billion electron volts — and to present the first serious estimate of the proton lifetime, the average time it takes for a proton to decay. Just on the basis of Heisenberg's uncertainty principle, which accounts for the suppression of the rate for nuclear beta-decay by a factor g_w^4/m_w^4, the rate for proton decay was expected to be much more strongly suppressed, by a factor g^4/m_x^4. Our analysis, which led to a more refined estimate of θ_w, also found a value for g of about $\frac{1}{2}$ and masses m_X for X and Y of roughly 20 trillion trillions of electron volts, which suggests a proton lifetime of about a billion trillion trillions of years, 10 thousand times longer than the experimental lower limit at the time. (For readers of *The Hitchhiker's Guide to the Galaxy*: we actually found for the associated "fine structure constant," which directly determines the probability for something to happen, $\alpha_{GUT} = g^2/4\pi = 1/42$.) We did a careful analysis of proton decay, using methods that had been developed for studying weak decays of strange particles, and found a further

---

[12] Neutrinos are massless in the Standard Model. There has been evidence that they might have very small masses since the late 1960s, but this was not firmly established until around 2000. Other evidence for physics beyond the Standard Model comes in the form of nonluminous matter ("dark matter") in galactic halos, which has been known about since the early 1930s, but was not established to be a new form of matter until the early 21st century.

A hike in the Caucasus Mountains.

suppression of the decay rate, and consequently a longer lifetime, by a factor of a hundred to a thousand. However subsequent measurements of the QCD coupling constant g_s converged on a lower value than we had used, bringing down the value of m_X by a factor 10, and thus decreasing the predicted lifetime by a factor of ten thousand, within reach of experimental detection. Although the average time it takes a proton to decay was predicted to be far, far longer than the age of the universe, if you watched a very large number of protons for a sufficiently long time, you would be able to detect some decays. So two mines were excavated to be filled with water that would be monitored for signs of these decays. One was the Kamioka zinc mine in Japan, and the other was the Morton Salt Mine, very close to my home town of Painseville (and right next to the beach where I used to swim in Lake Erie). On a visit to my cousins in Cleveland I took one of them with me to tour the site, took a turn at running the digging machine, and came home with a paperweight in the form of a lump of salt. However no proton decays were observed, and the Georgi–Glashow model was eventually ruled out. But for their trouble the two experiments were in an excellent position to make detailed studies of Supernova 1987A.

Unrest: Annecy

Although our work was widely cited, and I was invited to give many talks, I began to feel increasingly uncomfortable with my status as a sort of "permanent visitor" at CERN. John and I were mentoring a number of CERN Fellows; I even became the "official" mentor to one Fellow, Jan Finjord, when a mentoring policy was established in the theory group. So to get a different perspective on life I started spending summers, or parts of summers, at Fermilab, where I felt much more comfortably accepted as "a physicist." During most of these visits I had some or all of my children with me, and sometimes Jean-Marc joined us for part of the time. Once or twice my daughter Dominique had a summer job there as a gardener. Leon Lederman, by then the Director of Fermilab, loved to tell the story of how Dominique casually walked into his office during a meeting he was having with Erwin Schopper, the CERN Director-General, and asked (or rather demanded) to borrow 10 dollars. I also remember jogging around the main accelerator ring, sometimes with Dominique, sometimes with Leon, and once with my old Columbia classmate, Lillian Hartmann (now Lillian Hoddeson), who had become a respected historian of physics. Since we had about 15 years of our interim lives to recount, it was a very news-filled jog.

One summer there was a period of two or three weeks when I had no family with me in the small housing unit I had on the Fermilab site. I remember my mother worrying about me being all alone. But, in fact it was a welcome break from my multiple responsibilities, and I didn't have much time to get lonely, with many colleagues to interact with professionally and socially. During that period John Ellis came to Fermilab for a short visit and stayed in an extra room in my house. We were working on

With John Ellis at an ICFA meeting at Brookhaven in 1987.

contributions to the neutron electric dipole moment from both the electroweak interactions and from QCD effects.

Quantum effects in QCD allow for the brief appearance and disappearance of highly localized gluon fields. Configurations with both an "electric" and a "magnetic" gluon field in a rotationally invariant combination are not invariant under *P* or under *CP*. Their presence would in turn generate a large neutron electric dipole moment, in stark contradiction with experiment.

The neutron carries no net electric charge, but because it can emit and reabsorb electrically charged particles over very short time and distance scales, there are positive and negative charges distributed over a small area surrounding it. This means that it can interact with photons that are energetic enough to penetrate inside the radius of this charge distribution, about a hundredth of a trillionth of a centimeter. If the distribution is not uniform, but has electric charge increasing along some direction, invariance under rotations demands that this preferred direction must be parallel or antiparallel to the neutron spin. The dipole moment measures the average value of this non-uniformity. Under a parity reflection P along the spin axis, the spin itself does not change, but the direction of the charge distribution changes sign. Charge conjugation C does not affect it, so a non-vanishing dipole moment violates both P and CP conservation. The experimental data currently limits its absolute value to less than three hundredths of a trillionth of a trillionth of a centimeter in units of the positron charge.

Therefore it is generally believed that there is an additional spontaneously broken symmetry (called a Peccei–Quinn symmetry after Roberto Peccei and Helen Quinn, who first suggested it) that suppresses P and CP violating QCD effects. However, weak interactions are known to violate P and CP. John and I were studying the contributions to the dipole moment from weak interactions alone, as well as weak interaction corrections to the QCD contribution. We found that the GIM cancellation mechanism, generalized to include top and bottom quarks, is so effective that the result is compatible with the experimental limit, even if the energy where the new symmetry comes into play to suppress the QCD effects is much higher than the Planck energy of two million trillion electron volts, where new physics is expected because gravitational interactions become strong at this energy. During John's stay I went to visit my brother in Holland, Michigan. One night there was a violent storm in that part of the country, resulting in middle-of-the night revelations for both of us — me on how to handle the very large number of multiple interactions that we had to consider, and John on how to interpret the result. (I remember only one other time when I had a similar Eureka moment — sitting in a dentist chair in Berkeley — about a problem that I was working on with my students.)

The following year, the 1980 ICHEP conference was held at the University of Wisconsin in Madison, not far from Fermilab, where I was again spending part of the summer. So I attended the conference where I was planning to speak about work with John and Dimitri on a cosmological puzzle: why do we observe only protons, neutrons and electrons in ordinary matter, and not their antiparticles? According to the Big Bang theory, the universe started out as a hot dense plasma with quarks, leptons, their antiparticles and gauge bosons constantly interacting with one another. As the plasma cooled and the universe expanded, some of these interactions became ineffective when the interaction rate dropped below the expansion rate of the universe.

The interaction rate depends on the temperature, which is the average energy of the particles in the plasma, in units of the Boltzmann constant k. (Particle physicists typically use units in which $k = 1$, and I will do so here, just as for the velocity of light c and the Planck constant $\hbar$.) When this energy drops below the mass of some particle, that particle can no longer be produced and will disappear through decay or annihilation, as long as

In 1967, Andrei Sakharov delineated the conditions necessary for the origin of the observed matter–antimatter asymmetry in the universe.

- *There must be CP violation in the laws of physics. Otherwise for any process that increased the amount of matter over antimatter, there would be an equally probable process that did the opposite, and no asymmetry could be generated. Violation of charge conjugation C, which was known to be present in the weak interactions since the late 1950s, is also needed for the same reason. CP is the same as C except with all directions of motion reversed. Since particles in the hot plasma are moving in all directions with equal probability, the system is symmetric under parity P, so C conservation would also prohibit the development of an asymmetry.*
- *Baryon number B (the difference in the number of baryons and antibaryons) must also be violated because otherwise there would be no interactions that could change it and thereby create an asymmetry.*
- *There must have been a period in the history of the early evolution of the universe when the B and CP violating interactions were out of thermal equilibrium. This means that the probability for some physical state A to turn into a different state B is not the same as the probability for B to turn into A. Otherwise a net difference in baryon number would never be generated. For example, electron interactions drop out of equilibrium when the temperature of the plasma is lower than the electron mass. They still have time to annihilate with positrons into photons, but those energetic photons get separated in the expanding universe faster than they can recombine to make another electron–positron pair, and the energy of the bulk of photons in the plasma is too low to create such a pair.*

the rates for these processes exceed the rate of expansion. If there were equal numbers of baryons and antibaryons they would annihilate into mesons and photons. Later the mesons would decay or annihilate into leptons and photons, eventually leaving only photons, neutrinos and the lightest charged leptons — electrons and positrons — which would then annihilate into photons and neutrinos. There would be no matter, no galaxies and no people. This is hardly what we observe, so there must have been a time in the early history of the universe when there was a small difference between the number of baryons and antibaryons — small but considerably larger than what could have been generated by random fluctuations from equilibrium in the hot plasma.

CP violation has been known to be present in weak interactions since 1964. It was realized by many people that Grand Unified Theories, with their prediction of proton decay, provided both the needed baryon number violation and a non-equilibrium period: when the temperature dropped below the GUT-scale masses of the heavy gauge and scalar bosons, these bosons would decay into quarks and leptons, a no longer reversible process that could generate a net baryon (and lepton) asymmetry. John, Dimitri and I had shown that the simplest Georgi–Glashow GUT could not generate a sufficiently large matter–antimatter asymmetry, and we were looking for suitable modifications. When I started preparing the transparencies for my talk, I realized that for whatever new particles and interactions one added to the theory to increase the baryon asymmetry, there was a corresponding contribution to the electric dipole moment of the neutron. John and I had already found, for example, that if one embedded the Standard Model in that same Georgi–Glashow GUT, higher order corrections to the dipole moment became considerably larger, bringing down the needed energy scale of new physics, but leaving it still well above the Planck energy. However there was a clear tension between getting a large enough matter asymmetry and a small enough dipole moment, and I modified my talk accordingly. When I got back to CERN I found that John, Dimitri and Serge had been thinking along the same lines, and we wrote a paper setting a lower bound on the neutron dipole moment under the assumption that the matter asymmetry was generated by the decays of very heavy particles in a GUT. Aside from the fact that the anticipated decay of the proton as predicted by GUTs was not found, this mechanism is no longer considered the most likely source of the observed matter asymmetry because it is now believed that there was a period of very rapid expansion of the universe, called inflation, that would have diluted the asymmetry. After this period the universe would have reheated, but most probably would not have reached a temperature high enough to repopulate the universe with the heavy bosons needed to regenerate a matter–antimatter asymmetry. Other mechanisms for generating the asymmetry at lower temperatures have been suggested, and the origin of the asymmetry is still an open question.

There was also a summer when I had the less joyful activity of sorting through Ben's papers, since I was the only person Marianne trusted to do this. Among his papers were notes in my own handwriting on work that had been in progress with Ben on weak decays. I asked Marianne if I could take them. She at first said yes, but then called to tell me (to my astonishment — and scepticism) that her lawyer had advised against it because they might contain something valuable that Jon Rosner would also have a (monetary) right to. As far as I know, those papers are still sitting in Marianne's basement (although I was allowed to make copies of them).

As a visitor at CERN I was somewhat in limbo in more than one respect. One was the problem of students. CERN was a research laboratory, and as such its staff members did not advise students, although there were many student experimentalists who came with their advisors' groups to participate in collaborations among CERN and outside universities. As a member of the French CNRS, officially affiliated with the Orsay campus of the University of Paris, I could and did have a few students. The first was Guy de Teramond, now a Professor in Costa Rica and a sometime collaborator of Stan Brodsky at SLAC — so I run into him now and then. That was very early on in my career, and I think we only interacted during my trips to Paris. Much later, another Orsay student came to see me at CERN and I agreed to take him on. In the end it didn't work out — he had some psychological problems — but it was during his time with me that I realized I was in a lose-lose situation as far as students were concerned. In France (and more generally in Europe) at the time, there was a sort of patronage system. The various laboratories typically recruited the best of their own students to the exclusion of anyone else. This didn't lead to the optimal scientific outcome, but that's the way it was. Since I was no longer physically present at Orsay, except maybe for an occasional seminar, I wasn't considered one of them. I was pretty bluntly told that I had virtually no chance of placing a student at Orsay or anywhere else in France. So I took the only path possible; in 1979 I accepted an offer to start a new theory group at a recently established experimental laboratory in Annecy-le-Vieux, on the French side of the border with Switzerland, but on the other side of Geneva[13] from our home. At the time I had been sent a pre-Ph.D. student from Paris, by the name of Pierre Binétruy, to whom I was supposed to give a project. I had

---

[13] Geneva is essentially surrounded by France; I was once told that Geneva should be part of France, at least geographically, but is not because it is Protestant rather than Catholic.

misunderstood the nature of the assignment, which I think was roughly equivalent to a "reading course" here at Berkeley, in which the student reads up on a research topic and reports to his/her mentor weekly on her/ his progress. Instead I thought I was to give him a research topic for a *thèse de troisiéme cycle*, which I did, and which he completed successfully, unaware that that was what he was doing until it was finished. He eventually became my Ph.D. student, after some argument with the powers that be at *l'École Normale,* who wanted me to take one of their own. (Pierre had graduated from a lesser *École Normale*, outside of Paris.)

A parenthesis is in order here. During the political turmoil of the late 1960s and early 1970s, the laboratory in Orsay had split into three factions. The protests on campuses in the United States were mostly focused on specific issues like the Vietnam War and civil rights, while those in France had a lot more to do with perceived Marxist or, perhaps more accurately, Maoist ideology. This translated into the classroom, where students frowned on the "personality cult" in physics, in which certain people were lauded as giants in the field. On one of my visits to Orsay during that period, I was sharing an office with a professor who had committed the sin of talking about such heroes of physics. As a consequence, our office was occupied by a group of students for an hour or two. I don't remember how the offending professor was finally extricated, but I do remember that Claude Bouchiat came by, and he and I talked the students into an agreement according to which they would cease their occupation, and would be permitted to take their exams that had been disrupted by the protests. The following day Claude and I were admonished by the more conservative faculty (including my former advisor) for having even agreed to talk with the students. The end result was a three-way split of the Orsay group: the *gauchistes* (leftists), the conservatives (not very conservative by US standards, basically social democrats), and those who were more interested in doing physics than in their colleagues' political affiliations. (A similar split of a theory group along political lines took place at the Jussieu campus in Paris.) I was given the choice of joining one of these groups. My natural affinity was with the third group, but I did not want to offend my former advisor, so I declined to choose, which meant that I no longer went regularly to Orsay. The third, apolitical, group later moved to *l'École Normale* in the Paris Latin

Quarter, and these were the people with whom I remained most in scientific contact.

So Pierre became the first student in the theory group at LAPP (*Laboratoire d'Annecy-le-Vieux de Physique des Particules*), and a founding member, along with Georges Girardi and Paul Sorba (neither of whom were from either of the two preeminent Parisian *Grandes Écoles*). We were soon joined by Patrick Aurenche, who became the thesis advisor to one of the students from the Moroccan school where I had been with my son Bruno. We were promised funding for a kick-off conference by the LAPP director, Marcel Vivargent. But when the time came to start organizing it, it turned out that Vivargent had forgotten to set aside the funds for it. So as not to renege on his promise, he got me to open a personal bank account — which essentially amounted to a money laundering device.

It was standard French practice at the time to pay scientific visitors and conference attendees in bills of French francs, pinned together in bunches of a thousand, or something like that, in order to evade arcane regulations. When I left my stay at *l'École Polytechnique* as a 19 year old, somebody had decided that I should be recompensed for my efforts, and that's how it was done. Some 30 years or so later, I was still getting travel reimbursements the same way. I think those days have ended by now.

I opened an account with some trepidation, but there were no adverse consequences, and the conference was a success, with notables such as Shelly Glashow participating. As for Pierre, he eventually moved to a professorship at the Orsay campus of the University of Paris, and, as well as serving on many important French committees, later became the head of a cosmology center at a new Paris campus of the university.

1979 was also the year I gave plenary talks at two major biannual conferences: the Lepton–Photon conference at Fermilab, where I spoke about electroweak interactions, and the European ICHEP conference in Geneva, where I spoke about QCD. The theory session at Fermilab consisted of three speakers: the bushy-bearded collaborator of mine, John Ellis, the short-statured, preppy-looking (future Nobelist) Frank Wilczek and myself. John reported that he heard a Japanese "elder statesman" in our field remark somewhat in disgust: "A woman, a hippie and a school boy!" The previous year the very prestigious biannual

International Conference on High Energy Physics was held in Tokyo. This was part of the conference series that included Vienna in 1968, where I had served as a scientific secretary, Fermilab in 1972, where I had been a session organizer, and London in 1974, where I had gained some notoriety. It is the one major conference at which I never was a plenary speaker. One of the organizers of the Tokyo meeting, Yoshio Yamaguchi, told Jacques Prentki that he wanted me give the plenary talk on Grand Unified Theories. This would have been a big deal for me, a definitive sign that I was accepted as "a physicist." However Jacques also told me that the Tokyo people could not pay for foreign travel, even for invited speakers, and had asked CERN to pay. Jacques mumbled something to the effect that they could not pay for my travel because I was not a CERN employee. I was later told by my husband Jean-Marc that the French experimentalist Paul Falk-Variant, who was the CERN Research Director at the time, *"t'a rayée de la liste"* (excised you from the list of CERN delegates). Then came the comedy of errors. The same year, just before the Tokyo conference, there was to be a memorial conference for Ben Lee. It was obvious that my participation was of prime importance, but someone had to pay for my travel. It was clear that Orsay would not do so, so I appealed to Jacques. He finally OK'd it, provided I find the cheapest way to go. I went to the CERN Wagon-Lits office to explore the possibilities. I had been scheduled to spend part of the summer at Fermilab with my son Bruno. I ended up flying to JFK to put Bruno (who was very unhappy with the turn of events) on a direct flight to Geneva, and then flying to Seoul via Anchorage on KAL Flight 007, the very one that was shot down by the Soviets four years later. Sometime after this had all been arranged, somebody else at Wagon-Lits said he could have gotten me a much cheaper, and simpler, around-the-world trip.

When I arrived (exhausted) in Seoul and tried to register at the hotel, I was asked "where is your husband?" With some effort, I convinced the man behind the desk to look at the list of conference speakers and find my name, so he finally let me have a room. That was the first example of the generally sexist treatment I endured during my time in Korea, much to the embarrassment of my friend Wonyong Lee. Wonyong was a Columbia professor whose family had skied with ours in Verbier on several occasions. He gave many fascinating glimpses of the city to another colleague, Tim O'Halloran, and myself, including a dinner at the home of his mother, who cooked hamburgers so as not to shock our Western pallets. (I must admit the spiciest meal I ever had was in the cafeteria of Seoul University, where I had to give up on the squid as soon as my beer bottle was empty.) The day before I was scheduled to leave Korea, I got a phone call informing me that I had (once again) been bumped off my plane. Wonyong went with me to the travel agency and said something in Korean to the woman behind the desk, after which she asked me: "What is your major?" and issued me a boarding pass.

What was to have been a conference organized by Ben Lee had become a conference in his memory. He had been sent to Korea a couple of years earlier by the State Department to help set up a cooperative arrangement aimed at improving South Korean higher education in science. The conference had been planned as an integral part of that effort. However, such luminaries as Leon Lederman and Abdus Salam were there in part to carry on Ben's efforts, and met with the appropriate Korean authorities. (Salam's Nobel Prize had been announced when I was in Morocco, to the delight of our Muslim friends — who were at the same time puzzling over what an Ayatollah was, since that was also the period of the Iranian occupation of the US embassy.) They, like most of the Western participants in the Seoul conference, were on their way to Tokyo. So it added particular insult to injury when CERN staff member Daniele Amati approached me just after my complicated travel plans had been arranged. He told me that Guido Giuliano had given up his place as a CERN delegate; would I like to go in his place? In other words, CERN was now willing to pay me to go as a simple delegate, while they had refused to finance my trip as a principle speaker. This was a bit too much to stomach. As it turned out, Daniele was the session chair who was to introduce me for my plenary talk at Fermilab the following summer. I remember wondering what he would cite as my affiliation. Fortunately for everyone, he said "Annecy"; if he had cited CERN I might have had an unpleasant reaction. For all I know, Daniele may have been an innocent bystander in what was becoming a very traumatic and troubling experience for me.

I had (rather passively) been looking elsewhere for some time. Starting back in 1974, Ben had told me that I deserved a better position. At his instigation, Jean-Marc and I spent a day with the physics department of the University of Illinois at Chicago Circle. Nothing ever came of it — I'm not sure why, because given the status of high energy physics there at the time, we should have been considered something of a "catch." Even if we had gotten an offer, I'm pretty sure Jean-Marc would not have wanted to accept, and I wasn't especially enthusiastic about the place myself, with its rather gloomy architecture and somewhat mediocre particle physics, which we were supposed to inject new life into. A year or two later, Ben made an unsuccessful attempt to get the Fermilab theory group to hire me. Sometime in the late '70s the idea arose that Jean-Marc and I might move to the University of Marseille, which had an excellent theory group dominated by the mathematical physicist Daniel Kästler, the son of Alfred Kästler (and, like Orsay and Jussieu, was split into two politically antagonistic factions). The university was planning to establish a strong experimental effort as well. So we spent a couple of days in Luminy in the heart of the Calanques — sheltered inlets running between Marseille and Cassis, with high cliffs, *les falaises*, towering above. I mostly remember walking along the *falaises* with Daniel chattering enthusiastically about physics ideas, which I probably wouldn't have understood even if his words hadn't been drowned out by the *mistral* (strong north wind) that was removing bobby pins, one by one, from my improvised "up-do," until my long hair was blowing wildly with the wind. Again nothing further came of our visit.

In 1979, the same year that I started the group at Annecy, I was appointed to the Marseille theory group visiting committee for the duration of my time in France. We listened to presentations from the various areas of particle theory. Among the speakers was Daniel in his always enthusiastic form, repeating after each new concept something to the effect of: "It's so simple even your mother (*ta mère*) can understand it," with me muttering "*ton père*" (your father) under my breath each time. At one meeting of this committee, during a particularly obtuse and/or boring talk, I managed to solve a math question that I needed for a physics problem I was working on: if you have a number N of objects, how many different ways can you arrange another number n of them into symmetric combinations? The answer for the anti-symmetric case is fairly simple and is known to most physicists. The answer for the symmetric case has probably been known to mathematicians for a long time, but I couldn't find it anywhere in the literature. So during that presentation I worked out an elegant, if I may say so, solution using integration in the complex plane (which means that the x-axis — the horizontal axis or abscissa — represents real numbers, and the y-axis — the vertical axis or ordinate — represents imaginary numbers). Unfortunately, in the resulting paper, I wrote the answer only for $N = 70$, which was what I needed at the time. I lost my scribbled notes and never remembered exactly how I got the general solution.

I think it was sometime in 1978, probably during one of my summer visits, that a serious offer materialized from Leon Lederman, by then the director of Fermilab. He made a concurrent offer to Jean-Marc, who was, as always, reluctant to leave France. For reasons that I never quite comprehended, our friend Bjorn Wiik (who at some point — with Jean-Marc strongly objecting — wanted to hire me as the "hero" who would revitalize the theory group at DESY, after he had been turned down by John Ellis and Alvaro de Rujula) advised us that this was not the "right time" for us to move to the US. But the offer from Leon remained open.

Superguts

Meanwhile I was commuting two or three days a week to Annecy. Pierre, Georges and Paul had moved to Annecy, which is indeed a delightful place to live, as I learned myself when Bruno Zumino and I spent a month or two there after our move to Berkeley. But in 1979, my family and I had no incentive to move, since our lives were strongly rooted in the Geneva area. Often I drove with a contingent of collaborators, including John Ellis and Bruno Zumino, who, with Julius Wess, had discovered supersymmetry in four dimensions in 1974.

The possible relevance of supersymmetry to particle physics became recognized in the early 1980s when it was realized that it might solve what is known as the gauge hierarchy problem of the Standard Model. The problem is the very small value of the electroweak symmetry breaking energy v, as compared with the GUT energy V (or the Planck energy m_P) by a factor of a trillion (or a thousand trillion). Supersymmetry provided a technical solution to this dilemma in the sense that if one simply imposed this hierarchy of energy scales, it would not be spoiled by the effects of multiple interactions, because the extra symmetry provides new contributions from "superpartners" that cancel the Standard Model contributions, which, by themselves, should destroy the observed hierarchy of energy scales. This solution requires that the energy scale of supersymmetry breaking be no more than a factor 10 or so above the scale of electroweak symmetry breaking.

However, in 1980, John Ellis, Luciano Maiani, Bruno Zumino and I (EGMZ) were thinking about supersymmetry breaking near the Planck energy, since there was no evidence in nature for supersymmetric partners of the Standard Model particles. (The first hint came in 1991, when the value of the weak mixing angle θ_W was found to disagree significantly with the GUT prediction, but was consistent with the supersymmetric extension of the simplest GUT theory if one included supersymmetric partners with masses in the range of 10 to 1000 billion electron volts.) We were motivated by the idea of going beyond the "Grand Unification" of the three forces that are probed by accelerator experiments to a "Super Grand Unified Theory" (Supergut) that included gravity, and also by several recent theoretical developments.

SUPERSYMMETRY

Ordinary symmetries like isospin, or the electroweak and strong interaction gauge symmetries, interchange particles of different flavors or colors, with the same spin. By contrast, supersymmetry interchanges particles that differ in spin by one half unit. Therefore, the minimal supersymmetric extension of the Standard Model has twice as many matter particles and gauge particles as does the Standard Model. For each quark q and lepton l, with spin $\frac{1}{2}$, there is a companion "squark" $\tilde{q}$ and "slepton" $\tilde{l}$ with the same flavor and color quantum numbers, but with spin 0. For each gauge boson g with spin 1, there is a corresponding "gaugino" $\tilde{g}$ with spin $\frac{1}{2}$. The Standard Model Higgs boson H also requires a supersymmetric partner: a "Higgsino" $\tilde{H}$. However, if, for example, we associate the Higgs scalars H^+ and H^0 with two left-spinning fermions $\tilde{H}^+$ and $\tilde{H}^0$, the antiparticles of the scalars, namely H^- and $\bar{H}^0$, have as supersymmetric companions right-spinning antifermions $\tilde{H}^-$ and $\tilde{\bar{H}}$. Then the condition, discussed on page 50, that the electric charges of fermions and of antifermions sum to zero *separately* no longer holds. Therefore one has to

---

(Continued)

(Continued)

introduce *four* Higgs scalars: , H_u^+, H_u^0, H_d^0 and H_d^-, accompanied by four left-spinning Higgsinos, $\tilde{H}_u^+$, $\tilde{H}_u^0$, $\tilde{H}_d^0$ and $\tilde{H}_d^-$, and their antiparticles, with opposite charges and spins. It turns out that the quarks with charge $\frac{2}{3}$, like the up quark u, get masses from couplings to H_u^0, and those with charge $-\frac{1}{3}$, like the down quark d, get masses from couplings to H_d^0. There are now eight Higgs spin-0 particles, three of which get "eaten" to become the extra (third) spin-components of the massive $W^\pm$ and Z, so there are five left over. If the energy where supersymmetry is broken is sufficiently higher than that for electroweak symmetry breaking, the lightest of these has properties almost identical to the single Higgs particle of the Standard Model.

The first new development involved what is called "extended" supersymmetry, and is characterized by the number N of different supersymmetry operations, each of which can raise or lower a particle's spin by half a unit, without changing its color or flavor. In well-defined theories like the gauge theories of the Standard Model, spin is no larger than one. Then the spin component of a massless particle along its direction of motion may take integer or half-integer values in the range from 1 to -1, and the largest possible value of N is 4. It turns out that at most one supersymmetry can be present at energies not far above the scale of electroweak symmetry breaking in a supersymmetric extension of the Standard Model; this is the only possibility that allows different couplings for left- and right-spinning fermions.

Supersymmetry interchanges bosons and fermions, so the supersymmetry operator carries a half unit of spin, and behaves like a fermion, in that a product of different operators can appear only in an antisymmetric combination. It is a two-component operator, with one component Q that lowers the spin along some direction by a half unit, and another component $\bar{Q}$ that raises it by the same amount. For example if Q turns a massless scalar into a massless left-spinning fermion f, it also turns the right-spinning antifermion $\bar{f}$ into the scalar's antiparticle; $\bar{Q}$ effects the reverse transformations. In extended supersymmetry there is a set of N operators Q_i and the corresponding $\bar{Q}_i$. The index i denotes a new quantum number that is present in extended

> *supersymmetry theories; it takes integer values from 1 to N. Because of the antisymmetry condition, one cannot apply the same Q_i twice, so starting from a massless particle with a spin component along its axis of motion equal to some value S, one can apply up to N supersymmetry operators Q_i, generating a set of states with spin components ranging from S to S − N/2.*

Including gravity in a supersymmetric theory necessarily entails supergravity, the supersymmetric extension of Einstein's theory that was discovered in 1976 by Sergio Ferrara, Dan Freedman and Peter van Neuwenheusen, and by Stanley Deser and Bruno: the graviton, the particle associated with the gravitational field, acquires its own superpartner, a spin $-\frac{3}{2}$ fermion called the gravitino. In this case we have spin as high as two, so spin components can take values from 2 to −2, and the largest value of N is 8. Supergravity theories are not well defined by the commonly understood definition. However with each new symmetry there are more cancellations of higher order effects. For example, it was speculated that $N = 4$ supersymmetry might actually be finite, meaning that one could just calculate anything, and get a sensible, testable result, in terms of the input parameters of the theory (in this case just specifying the value of the gauge coupling constant), rather than having to rely on *measured* parameters before a sensible answer can be obtained, which is the case for the "well-defined" theories of the Standard Model. This theory was in fact proven to be finite in 1987 by our Berkeley colleague, Stanley Mandelstam. Stanley, who was already famous for his work on scattering theory, was so modest that nobody in our group knew that he had made this discovery until John Schwarz came to visit our department. I met John in the hallway, coming out of Stanley's office, and he told me that he had asked Stanley what he was working on. The answer was no less than this very important result.

This suggested that, with sufficient symmetry, it was possible that all the troublesome multiple interactions in supergravity might just cancel out, giving a finite theory. This had been conjectured at the time for $N = 8$ supergravity, with counter-examples occasionally cropping up and then disappearing. The issue is still not settled, although evidence that this theory is finite seems to be mounting. This made it a tantalizing candidate for a "Theory of Everything." The first to seriously entertain this possibility was Murray Gell-Mann, who found however that the elementary states in the theory do not include all the particles of the Standard Model, so one would have to conclude that some Standard Model particles, including the heavy Ws and Z, as well as some quarks and leptons, were bound states of the elementary states. Our approach was even more radical, and drew on a 1979 result of Eugène Cremmer and Bernard Julia.

Each extended supergravity theory is invariant under transformations among the N supersymmetry operators Q. A subset of these transformations are rotations in an N-dimensional abstract space, and the number of vector bosons is the same as the number of independent angles needed to specify these rotations. As a consequence, the rotational invariance can be promoted to a gauge invariance, with the vector bosons as gauge bosons. This was the approach that Murray had investigated. However, the version of the theory without this gauge invariance has a much larger symmetry, which had been found by Cremmer and Julia. This larger symmetry allows for the possibility of gauging the full symmetry of transformations among the Qs, provided the associated gauge bosons, as well as fermions and scalars, are *all* bound states of the elementary particles of the theory. In this way we obtained all the particles of the Standard Model as well as a whole lot more. The way we got rid of the "whole lot more" was using something we called "Veltman's theorem."

One day Bruno and I were having lunch with Tini Veltman, and we broached the subject as to whether one can argue that in order for a theory to make sense below some energy scale, it had to look like a mathematically consistent theory below that energy. Tini gave us a convincing argument as to why this was a reasonable supposition, so I suggested that we dub the conjecture "Veltman's theorem," in part because Tini himself had named some of his own inventions after his friends Jacques Prentki and John Bell. (John deservedly had something of his own named after him, namely Bell's theorem, that afforded tests of the very foundations of quantum mechanics, and for which he unwittingly became something of a cult hero in California in the 1970s.) However nobody seemed to understand the connection to Tini's practice; for example Murray Gell-Mann asked: "But then what did you do?" (Actually, as we later learned, similar arguments had been put forth earlier by several other people.) Anyway, applying this "theorem," we were able to show that

(1) we could obtain all the Standard Model particles as bound states, (2) the unique unifying gauge theory for the strong and electroweak interactions was the Georgi–Glashow theory, and (3) there were precisely three "families" of quarks and leptons, that is, three sets with identical electroweak and color quantum numbers. For example, the lightest family consists of u, d, e, v_e. I presented the EGMZ paper at a conference in Erice, Sicily, and it appeared in the proceedings. John, Bruno and I went on to write a couple more papers on this scenario, including one with Murat Günaydin (who had been a student of my father's at what was then Robert College in Istanbul) on more mathematical aspects of the full symmetry of the theory.

The EGMZ paper had found the entire set of bound states that transform into one another under supersymmetry transformations and gauge transformations, and that contain all the Standard Model particles. However the full symmetry of the theory is much larger, with additional symmetry operations similar to chiral transformations in QCD, which turn a state into another one by adding or removing a pion. In the case of $N = 8$ supergravity, the full symmetry demanded that we had to complete the bound state multiplets by including additional states made from the original ones by adding any number of the 70 elementary scalars of $N = 8$ supergravity — in symmetric combinations — ad infinitum, which was why in that meeting in Marseille I had worked out the way to do it. Later, after Bruno and I had moved to Berkeley, I presented my results at a 1982 math conference in Chicago and wrote up my talk for publication in the proceedings. I had been thinking about this while I was still at CERN, and had many discussions with Murray Gell-Mann, who was approaching the issue of symmetry completion along a different line. When my preprint appeared, he was rather put out and called me to say I should withdraw it, and we should write a different paper together. Since Murray had a reputation for getting younger people to work with him and then postponing publication of the results until he was certain everything was to his satisfaction (which sometimes meant never), I preferred to let my paper stand as it was. In any case the math and the methods were correct. However Murray and Yuval Ne'eman then complained that the methods I had used had been invented by them.

Left: Women at Shelter Island in 1983 (including Helen Quinn, Nina Byers, So Young Pi and Louise Dolan). Right: with Alain and with Dominique on a 1985 trip to China arranged at the same conference by Tsung Dao Lee and Zhou Guangzhao.

The issue surfaced again at the Second Shelter Island Conference off Long Island, NY, in early June, 1983 (the original Shelter Island Conference in 1947 had provided an explosion of important results in the development of quantum field theory). It came in the midst of the very painful deliberations of a DOE committee I was serving on, and those of us attending had to fend off inquisitive reporters, as well as intense pressure from high-powered interested parties. It also, unusually for that period, had seven women invitees, essentially all the women particle theorists then working in the US. The most senior among us suggested that we take advantage of this occasion to discuss some of the issues facing women in physics. We sat together on the lawn during a lunch hour, to the outrage of one of the organizers who felt he had done a great thing for women by inviting us all, and took our gathering together as some kind of affront. I pointed out to him that there were groups of as many men sitting around.

Getting back to superunification, Bruno gave a talk at Shelter Island in which he mentioned my work, and pointed out the difference (something about "expansion" as opposed to "decontraction" of a group of operations) of the method I had used from that of Gell-Mann and Ne'eman, who were both in the audience and raised some objections. The written version of Bruno's talk avoided controversy by omitting the subject altogether, and I added references to the (unpublished) Gell-Mann–Ne'eman work and to other earlier literature in the 1985 published version of my math conference talk.

In the end, we were never were able to derive the Standard Model interactions in this picture, and we eventually abandoned it in favor of string theory, which later became much more fashionable. There were, however, some unanticipated consequences of our endeavor.

In December of 1980, not long before my move to Berkeley, I was the Loeb lecturer at Harvard. John Hagelin, a Ph.D. student of Howard Georgi, was then dating my cousin Holly Manon. Earlier in his Ph.D. studies, Howard had asked him to study the write-up of a course on weak decays of heavy quarks that I had given at a SLAC summer school, and he was anxious to meet me. I arranged to have dinner with Holly and John on a Sunday evening, after a weekend car trip to Maine to visit my former teacher and mentor Dorothy Montgomery, by then remarried. It was the last time I saw her, but I developed a friendship with her husband, Tom Johnson, a former cosmic ray physicist who was interested in learning about modern particle physics, and we remained in contact for a number of years. I had rented a supposedly bargain car from a place recommended by the Harvard physics department (I was a temporary faculty member by virtue of my appointment as a Loeb lecturer). It didn't seem all that cheap, and was not equipped for winter, as I learned when snow started falling just as I was leaving Dorothy's house. I immediately skidded, and afterward very slowly drove — or often glided — my way back to Cambridge, arriving probably an hour late for dinner. But Holly and John were waiting for me and we had a pleasant dinner with John explaining to me how he reconciled the laws of physics with the powers of transcendental meditation. The last of my four lectures was on our approach to superunification, and I explained in detail the particle content and the symmetries of $N = 8$ supergravity. John copied all my slides, and not long afterwards a poster appeared featuring this theory as the Maharishi's view of the unified field, incorporating not just unification of the four forces familiar to particle physicists, but human consciousness as well. The poster hung on a wall of our home in Berkeley for a number of years. Like ourselves, John later gave up on $N = 8$ supergravity as the Theory of Everything, and espoused a particular version of superstring theory. He moved to the Maharishi International University (now Maharishi University of Management), and twice ran for President on the Natural Law Party ticket.

Much later, in the mid-1990s, I was being vetted for an appointment to the National Science Board, which like the National Science Foundation that it oversees, is not part of a cabinet department, but reports directly to the President, and Science Board members, as well as the NSF director, require Senate confirmation. Besides an FBI investigation, there was a call from the White House legal office to determine whether I had ever done anything that "might embarrass President Clinton" (which struck me as something of an oxymoron). I remember only three questions. Did I have a nanny problem? I thought that I didn't, since my children were grown and had all been raised in Europe. But it turns out that "nanny" is more broadly defined, including house cleaners, that not only have to have green cards or citizenship, but for whom the employer is supposed to pay taxes, a provision of the law that almost nobody knew about. (The law has since been relaxed.) The end result was that I ended up paying about five years in back taxes (the fine was waived), one check for each quarter. This came to 20 payments, many of which turned out to be over-payments, so I regularly got checks back for amounts on the order of five or ten cents, each in a separate envelope bearing a first class stamp (around 30 cents at the time) — not a very efficient way to collect taxes.

The other two "questions" were more like statements. First, I had signed a letter to the editors of several newspapers supporting the SSC. (This was in 1993, following the "Year of the Woman," with six women Senators for the first time, and our letter was originally sent to all the women members of Congress, as well as then Secretary of Energy Hazel O'Leary, and signed by 125 women particle physicists, but only the signatures of one or two of us who had organized the effort appeared in the papers.) My response was simply that I still believed that the SSC should have been built (and I still do). Secondly, Haim Harari had written a Scientific American article on models with composite quarks. He included a mention of the EGMZ paper, which he described as "ambitious," but "like other composite models… has serious flaws." To this I responded that we no longer believed in the theory ourselves.

More importantly for physics, Bruno and I had written a paper (the one we dedicated to Andrei Sakharov) that was originally intended to address the question as to whether it was possible for gauge bosons to appear as massless bound states in $N = 8$ supergravity. Cremmer and Julia had speculated that this could happen, based on results by Alessandro d'Adda, Paolo Di Vecchia and Martin Lüscher, who had studied a theory with just one spatial dimension, but which had a symmetry structure similar to (but much simpler than!) that of extended supergravity theories. They found a composite spin-one bound state which was the gauge boson of an Abelian gauge symmetry (like QED). For every gauge boson there is a symmetry operation, which implies the existence of a corresponding conserved quantum number, as was shown by Emmy Noether in 1915. For example, QED with one gauge boson, the photon, conserves electric charge, and QCD with eight gluons has eight conserved quantum numbers, two of which simply ensure that the net color of the particles in an interaction does not change. Supergravity theories with four or more supersymmetry operators include symmetry operations that interchange electric and magnetic fields (or, equivalently, interchange left-spinning and right-spinning vector bosons). To address the question of conserved quantum numbers, Bruno and I constructed the most general class of theories with this electric–magnetic symmetry. We indeed found the conserved quantum numbers, and our paper turned out to have important applications in superstring theory, which soon eclipsed $N = 8$ supergravity as the prime candidate for the "Theory of Everything," because it is known to be finite (again, formally proven by Stanley Mandelstam in 1992) and offers the possibility of generating the particle content of the Standard Model — in this picture "particles" are actually the lowest vibrational modes of very tiny strings. Our results have also been used by Renata Kallosh as part the on-going effort to determine whether $N = 8$ supergravity is finite.

Meanwhile, discontent with my situation at CERN was becoming more intense. Alain passed his *bac* (baccalaureate) in the summer of 1979, two years ahead of his sister Dominique because he had skipped a grade very early on. In his last year of school he and his friends had become somewhat rebellious, fancying themselves as anarchists of a sort, and turning in work that mocked the teaching methods of at least one instructor. As a consequence, not only were they told they could not return to the Ferney *Lycée* if they did not pass the *bac*, but their younger siblings were also refused readmission. As a result, Dominique spent her last two years of high school at a private international school in Switzerland (where she became good friends with Pascale Mompoint, who later became Alain's wife). Along with unusually high salaries, CERN staff members had a number of additional perks, including tuition for private schooling. By that point in my life, I was bold enough to announce to Jacques Prentki, the theory group leader at the time, that I would no longer spend any time at CERN without some financial help.

So for two years I became for the first time a (partially) paid visitor at CERN. But Jacques had a curious world view. Jean-Marc and I had a dinner party that included Murray Gell-Mann and Jacques as guests. At some point in the conversation Jacques made a comment something to the effect that woman can't do theoretical physics, which prompted Murray to tell him he needed a new pair of glasses. On another occasion I was having lunch at CERN in the company of Jacques and Dave Jackson (who was later responsible for getting me to Berkeley) and Jacques was talking about the need to hire senior staff members who were sufficiently young (the implication being that I was too old), to which Dave responded "not if the person is a woman." As it turns out, Alvaro De Rujula, who is a year or two younger than I, was hired a year or two later, in other words at the same age I was when this conversation took place. The rationale in his case was that his career was delayed by military service — but a delay in one's career due to babies didn't count.

I don't remember what occasioned it, perhaps a woman candidate being denied a CERN Fellowship, but the theory group called a staff meeting about women, to which I was invited, as well as the theory secretaries. Among other things the subject of military service versus child care was discussed. Towards the end of the meeting someone, perhaps Alvaro, said that women don't face any more obstacles than men do, and I replied that I could write an essay on the subject. As we were leaving the meeting John Bell asked me: "Why don't you?" and the Report on Women in Scientific Careers at CERN (CERN/DG-11) was born. This was a joint effort that appeared on March 8 (International Women's Day) in 1980. The first meeting included many of the women physicists at CERN as well as other technical and administrative personnel. Two older women, experimentalists whose experimentalist husbands were senior staff members, attended only that first meeting, probably for fear of rocking the boat. They also had permanent positions, albeit as "lab staff," which did not allow the scientific independence of the regular research staff. We devised a questionnaire that was sent out to all the women in scientific and technical positions at CERN. The report included data provided to us by the personnel office and the results of our survey, as well as some personal comments and reflections. There was an appendix on our unsuccessful attempt to expand the CERN nursery school to an all-day child care facility to better serve the women working at CERN. We were told that this could happen only if a sufficient number of children were enrolled in advance to insure financial solvency. This was not an easy task, given the time-frame we had to enlist enrollees. My daughter Dominique and I, together with our friend Shiela McGarry, a member of the CERN secretariat and a prime mover in the effort, spent a Saturday putting posters around CERN to announce the event. The following Monday, they were all

CERN/DG-11
8 March 1980

REPORT ON WOMEN IN SCIENTIFIC CAREERS AT CERN

Mary K. Gaillard

LAPP, Annecy, France
and
CERN, Geneva, Switzerland

angrily torn down by a member of the administrative staff because, he said, we had not gone through the proper procedures to get permission for putting up posters. Nevertheless we had nine students enrolled by June of 1979 for a planned start-up in September when the Executive Committee of the Staff Association voted to cancel the project. A similar effort was made at Fermilab during the same time-frame with the support of the Director (then Leon Lederman), and a subsidized all-day childcare center opened there in January of 1980 with initially only three children enrolled. Our report was distributed as a CERN report, with only the constraint that we move the cartoons from the front cover (as pictured here) to the inside of the cover. The Wolinski cartoon[14] (a woman had for the first time been elected to the prestigious *Académie Francaise*) was free, but the International Herald Tribune charged us 100 Swiss francs for Peanuts (Title IX had been strengthened). I asked Leon Van Hove, then the Director General, if CERN would pay for it; instead he took 20 francs out of his pocket and told me to take up a collection, which I did, asking a few other well-paid staff members to contribute.

The day after the staff meeting on women, Jurko Glaser, a senior staff member from Zagreb, told me in the lunch line that he had proof that women cannot do theoretical physics: Yugoslavia was a perfectly egalitarian socialist society, and there were no women theorists there. However the meeting did lead to some kind of lip service towards increasing gender diversity. I think Anne Davis became the first woman theory Fellow as a result, but Belen Gavela, who had been a student at Orsay and a postdoc at Annecy, was turned down. When I objected I was assured by Jacques Prentki that she would be taken the following year. However the selection took place while I was away, and Belen was rejected again. Her letters of support from me (another woman) and Alvaro (a fellow Spaniard) were discounted. This happened after most postdoc positions elsewhere were closed. By this time I already had an offer from Berkeley as well as from Fermilab, and I wrote a very strong letter of recommendation explaining the situation. In the end Belen got offers from Berkeley and Brandeis.

---

[14] There's a woman ... What? There's a woman at the Academy! Can't she wait until the end of the session to clean the room?

When she discovered the distance between the two coasts, she took the Brandeis offer to be closer to her husband.

Not long after I was invited to spend two weeks at Harvard as a Loeb lecturer in December of 1980, I also got an invitation to spend four weeks at Berkeley the following January as a Chancellor's lecturer. Since they both required four lectures, no extra work was involved, and I accepted. The Chancellor's lectureship was a position designated specifically for "underrepresented groups," with the aim of increasing diversity among the campus faculty. A female colleague called me to point this out, seemingly implying that I should not accept, but given the prestige of the Loeb lecture I felt no insult, and I already suspected that the people at Berkeley had something more in mind when they undertook this effort to introduce me to the physics faculty. Moreover, I learned that the author James Baldwin, whose work I had read and admired (and whom my father had befriended and defended when he was a visiting scholar at Robert College in Istanbul) had held the same appointment. This I learned when I complained to Dave Jackson about being asked to sign a loyalty oath, having been under the misunderstanding that this requirement had been abolished in the 1950s. Dave, who was then the physics department chair, told me that Baldwin had the same reaction, and please just sign it. This oath declared loyalty to the constitution of California, without requiring the denial of membership in subversive organizations that had been included in the version that was so controversial in 1949 — and that had cost the University many outstanding faculty.

I had planned to spend the holiday period between Harvard and Berkeley with my son Alain, who was a student at the University of Washington, including a week of skiing in Sun Valley with Leon and Ellen Lederman, along with Leon's old friend Isaac Halpern, then a professor at UW, and his wife Pat. As I was about to leave our house in Echenevex to catch my plane, Alain called to announce that he wouldn't be able to ski because he had fallen off a fence (after a few beers) and had broken both wrists. (I wasn't totally surprised, since he had always been accident-prone — the most frightening incident for me being the time he fell down the stairwell from the fourth floor at CERN. Just a few days before, he would have hit a lot of sharply edged metallic stuff in the basement, but fortunately somebody had boarded it up, and he suffered only a mild concussion.) When I arrived in Seattle, Alain picked me up at the airport and grabbed my suitcases with his two broken wrists. He said we should go to Sun Valley anyway, and since the weather in Seattle was wet and dismal, he suggested we first go to Berkeley. On New Year's Eve, he got me to drive him to the Oakland Coliseum where there was a Grateful Dead concert, but it had long since been sold out and there wasn't even room to camp outside the Coliseum. Then he left me sitting in the car in a parking lot, while he tried unsuccessfully to obtain a bit of an "illegal substance." With that misadventure over, we went back to our rented house and watched Benny Hill. He had brought along his skis ("just in case"), and when we got to Sun Valley he told me he would ski only the easy slopes. So I followed him to a lift that took us to the top of a very steep and bumpy slope; he plunged down it and immediately fell. He looked up at me with a bloody face but his hands in the air: "Look, Mom, I didn't land on my wrists." He continued skiing, and we had a pleasant drive back to Seattle with the Halperns.

At Berkeley, in addition to scientific lectures, I gave a talk about the status of women at CERN, and attended a potluck dinner, a monthly event organized by the women graduate students in physics. This effort was led at the time by Persis Drell, the daughter of a prominent theorist, Sidney Drell, and the dinner was at the home of another graduate student, Marjorie Shapiro. There had never been a woman on the Berkeley physics faculty, even though there were some outstanding women physicists at Lawrence Berkeley Laboratory, where, under the leadership of Luis Alvarez, a number of hadron states had been discovered, revealing the pattern of particle masses and quantum numbers that eventually led Gell-Mann and Zweig to hypothesize the existence of quarks. Alvarez had amassed a very large group. Most (or maybe all) of the men in that group also had professorships at the university, but not any of the women. I remember an ICHEP conference at which Sulamith Goldhaber was a plenary speaker, and I learned from the gossip that she was not a faculty member, although her husband Gerson was. At the time the gossip suggested that maybe she was the better of the two, although Gerson later played an important role in uncovering the existence of charmed particles. The group of women students was insistent about the need for at least one woman faculty member, and, as I understand it, browbeat Dave Jackson, then the chair, until he finally got me to Berkeley. As a result he was awarded a certificate conferring him with the status of "honorary woman." Persis went on to become a professor at Cornell, and later the Director of SLAC at Stanford. Marjorie joined the Berkeley faculty, after a stint at Harvard, and was the first woman chair of the department.

During my stay at Berkeley there was also a meeting of theorists in San Francisco, hosted by the "est" (Erhard Seminars Training) founder Werner Erhard. When he learned that I was in the Bay Area, he asked me to participate as much as my schedule allowed because he had "wanted to include a woman." It was a luxurious environment, but also a rather disturbing experience. The ever-smiling est trainees, who served us food and generally took care of us, gave me the impression of having been brainwashed, as I commented to Steve Weinberg at dinner. He apparently took the remark to heart, later stating that he would not attend another Erhard sponsored conference. I was seated between Steve and Shelly Glashow, both friends of mine, but not particularly friendly with each other. The same seating arrangement had been organized about a year earlier, when they visited CERN on their way back from the Nobel Prize ceremony in Stockholm — maybe I was there to keep the peace. The other issue that came up during my dinner conversation with Steve was the fact that — to his surprise — I was not a CERN staff member. Shortly thereafter he sent me a copy of an "unsolicited" (his word) letter to Jacques Prentki expressing the view that this was incomprehensible.

Fortunately for me, I was unable to attend the Erhard meeting the day the conference ended — I don't remember if the ending was on schedule or premature — because the press had gotten wind of it and the meeting concluded with the physicists being hustled out the back door.

In October of 1973, while I was at Fermilab, I had been promoted to the CNRS rank of *Maître de Research* (Research Master), which is roughly equivalent to a tenured position in a US university; the position carried no formal tenure, but rehiring was in practice automatic. A position for the highest level, as *Directeur de Research* (Research Director) was opening up starting in January of 1980. The Paris establishment was pushing someone from *l'École Normale*, but Raymond Stora, who had joined the Annecy theory group, and was president of the relevant CNRS committee, insisted, contrary to French custom, on asking for outside letters. At first I was told that I would get the promotion provided I committed to staying in France for five years. A colleague of mine had been promoted a couple of years earlier under a similar provision. I refused, but, thanks to the letters, I was promoted anyway.

When I returned to CERN in early 1981 after the lectures at Harvard and Berkeley, I began serving a term on the CERN SPS (Super Proton Synchrotron) Advisory Committee, and was also busy preparing the scientific program for a six-week summer school at Les Houches, near the town of Chamonix in the French Alps. A senior staff position in the CERN Theory Division was opening up. There were three candidates, including myself. Again contrary to custom, John Ellis and Bruno Zumino demanded outside letters. John had been offered a senior staff position as soon as he had gotten an offer for a position at SLAC. The same had happened with Chris Llewellen-Smith, who declined in favor of an Oxford professorship, but later became Director General of CERN. Gabriele Veneziano became a CERN senior staff member after he was offered a position at the University of California at Berkeley. I had been sitting on an offer from Fermilab for three years, and by now had an offer from Berkeley. But these offers held no sway with the majority of the CERN senior staff, nor did the letters.

CERN was simply "not ready to hire a woman," as one of my American colleagues put it. Shortly after I arrived in Berkeley, I was asked to speak at a conference in Memphis. At the conference banquet one of the attendees, whom I had not met before, asked: "How can you be good enough to get a job at Berkeley, but not good enough to get a job at CERN?" In 1984, my friend Belen Gavela, who is now a professor in Madrid, at last obtained a CERN Fellowship, and in 1989 a six-year junior staff position, becoming the first woman theorist on the CERN staff. (Although gender diversity was hardly a priority at CERN in the 1970s, national diversity was imperative, in the sense that all member countries had to be proportionally represented. At some point there was a perceived need for a German theorist, and the best candidate(s) were a couple, Barbara and Fridger Schrempp, who had always written papers together. One junior staff position was available. Since there was no way to distinguish between them scientifically, CERN let them decide who should get the position. It went to Fridger, with Barbara explaining that otherwise she would not know what to say to her mother-in-law.) In 1994, a senior staff position was awarded to Fabiola Gianotti, who as spokesperson for the ATLAS collaboration at the time of the July 4 announcement of the Higgs discovery, was a runner up for Time magazine's 2012 Person of the Year. Pippa Wells, who also has a leading role in the ATLAS experiment, became a CERN Fellow in 1990, and later in the '90s a CERN senior staff member as well. Since then there have been others, but none in theory as far as I know.

But by 1990, when Bruno Zumino and I were at CERN on a spring sabbatical leave, CERN had still not hired a female senior staff physicist. Our friends Andrei Linde and Renata Kallosh were also there, he as a staff member, and she as a "scientific associate," the same position I had held (in my case mostly unpaid) all those years. They are the couple with whom we had left Gorbachev's book when we visited Moscow after a conference in Armenia. We also left them our backpacks, and they gave us a lovely pair of tea cups and saucers, as well as extensive tours of the city — including a visit to the Novodevichy Cemetary, the burial grounds for many distinguished Russians (which was not open to the public at the time). Renata was well known for her work on field theory and supersymmetry; Andrei was the second father of "inflation." He had improved on the original version of inflation suggested by Alan Guth, who was the first to point out that certain puzzles in observational cosmology could be resolved if there was a period in the (very early) history of the

---

The universe as observed today is highly homogeneous when viewed over very large distances: it looks the same in all directions. This is expected for a region of space where light has had time to travel from one extremity to the other, allowing for interactions to smooth out inhomogeneities. However, light emitted early in the evolution of the universe reaches us today from regions so far apart that they could not have been in contact, unless the universe has at some time expanded far more rapidly than standard cosmology could account for, assuming it is filled with a gas of objects subject to the laws of thermodynamics and Einstein's general relativity. Such an expansion also has the effect of "flattening" the universe. Consider blowing up a balloon. As the radius of the balloon increases, a fixed area on the surface appears flatter:

> *measuring that area using rectilinear coordinates gives a more accurate result as it flattens. The fact that we can make accurate measurements (to an extremely high precision, as demonstrated in modern cosmological observations) using rectilinear coordinates for the three spatial dimensions we observe shows that our universe is flat, while the theory provides no reason why some or all of these dimensions should not be curled up with radii that could be as small as the Planck length of a billionth of a trillionth of a trillionth of a centimeter. Inflation provides the rationale for both the homogeneity and flatness of our universe. Inflation can occur if some scalar field acquires a very large value at some very early time.*

universe when space expanded at an exponentially fast rate; this period of rapid expansion is called inflation.

CERN was offering Andrei a permanent position, and suggested that Renata could get a position at Annecy. Renata commented that when she mentioned this to American colleagues, the response was: "We've heard this story before." However they were both being considered for professorships at Stanford. We talked with them about the advantages of not having to commute, and what turned out to be most important for them, not having a forced retirement age in the US, and still being able to continue on research grants and supervise graduate students even after retirement. We agreed to sponsor them for their visa applications and to write letters of recommendation to Stanford (pretty much a formality). Bruno took care of Renata's case, since she was an expert on supersymmetry and supergravity who had served as Bruno's scientific secretary when he had been a plenary speaker at an ICHEP conference in the Soviet Union. I sponsored Andrei; inflation was a subject I had worked on with Pierre Binétruy in the context of supergravity and superstring theory. In the fall of that year, Renata and Andrei became professors at Stanford.

After the CERN decision, it was clear to me that I would move to the United States. Throughout the spring and summer of 1981, I was agonizing over the choice between Fermilab and Berkeley. I was torn between loyalty to Leon, whose support and friendship had helped to sustain my morale over the years, and the attraction of becoming a professor at a leading university. My parents were visiting during the early part of the summer, and I remember eating Geneva's famous *filet de perches* with them in a café overlooking Lake Geneva. I showed them a letter from a faculty member, Somner Davis, urging me to go to Berkeley, and my mother (in spite of her own friendship with Leon) came down strongly on the side of Berkeley, I think because of the prestige it carried. Fermilab had the advantage of not having to teach (with the disadvantage of not having many students around) and also of being close to the experimental action. (As it turned out, I became very involved in the Fermilab physics program for many years anyway.) Many of the Fermilab senior staff held concomitant positions at one of the nearby universities, but the only one in the top-tier class, the University of Chicago, "was pretty much filled up," according to Leon. Berkeley had the advantage of access to first-rate students and — what I didn't really appreciate at the time — continuous learning through teaching and interacting with students. And then there were the women students who so badly wanted a role model. Leon tried to downplay this aspect, but as it turned out, during the first decade of my tenure at Berkeley there were only four women graduate students in theoretical particle physics; three of them were my students (the fourth was interested in more formal mathematical physics). For five years, until Marjorie Olmstead joined the faculty in 1986, I was the only woman faculty member available to attend the monthly potluck dinners with women graduate students; one of them was held at our house in the North Berkeley Hills, with my husband Bruno hiding out on the lower floor. Moreover, I was more attracted to the Bay Area with its liberal politics and "come as you are" attitude towards lifestyle than to the bucolic life of Batavia. John Ellis described Berkeley as my "natural habitat." Ellen and Leon rode horses, but I'm not a horse person, although Ellen did manage to get me on one, and even take a ride across the grounds once.

Sometime during that summer I got a call from a colleague at MIT, inquiring about my possible interest in a new chair for women, endowed by women alumnae. I didn't want to confuse things further, so I declined. There were also some attempts to keep me in France. I knew I had always been welcome to join the *École Normale* theorists, but things came full circle, ironically speaking, when I was asked about my interest in a professorship at *l'École Polytechnique*.

It was a very busy summer, largely occupied by preparations for the Les Houches summer school. About a year before, Maurice Jacob, a CERN senior staff member who was involved in the Les Houches program, had asked me to organize a session on High Energy Physics. Founded in 1951 by Cécile DeWitt-Morette, *l'École de Physique des Houches* had been the primary source of education for doctoral students during the many years before there was formal graduate instruction in the French university system. I was familiar with earlier sessions that had typically lasted for six weeks, and I developed a program accordingly. When I showed the proposal to Maurice, his initial reaction was that he had meant for me to organize only a two-week session, but when he saw the program I had devised and the roster of speakers I had enlisted (including Leon, who perhaps had accepted only as part of his effort to recruit me), he revised his schedule and my six-week program got the go-ahead. Then it became time to sort through the applicants. As far as I recall, this task fell to Maurice, myself and Raymond Stora, who for a number of years served as Administrative Director of the Les Houches school. There were many excellent candidates, including an outstanding cohort of women applicants. When we had finished the first ranking we ended up with 14% women, an astonishing number for the time. That is roughly the typical percentage of women graduate students in US physics departments today.[15] Someone asked if we should look at diversity issues, but we quickly decided that there was no need. I have no idea if the fact that a woman was scientific director was a factor in the large number of women applicants, but because of the critical mass that resulted, the women students played a leading role in the scientific activities at the school — a level of women's active participation that I had not seen before in particle physics. Overall, the six-week session turned out to be highly successful, both scientifically and socially.

---

[15] In 1993 when Sandra Cio-Cio and I were gathering women's signatures for a letter in support of the SSC, I got some AIP data which showed that in the early 1970s only 3% of physics Ph.D.s went to women. This number, which had remained nearly flat since I was a graduate student in the early 1960s, rose steadily in the 70s and 80s to over 10% at the time of our letter. Since then it seems to have leveled off again at around 15%.

Thirty-eight of the 51 young participants are still active in particle physics, including five of the seven women. Many of them have become leaders in our field, in terms of both scientific contributions and service to the high energy physics community.

When the school started on August 3, I had still not come to a decision about my future. By then my personal life had undergone a profound change: Jean-Marc and I were separated, and Bruno Zumino and I were together. Although Bruno had resisted my efforts (before we were even an "item") to enlist him as a lecturer (instead I got his long-time collaborator Julius Wess), he ended up attending the school as a "spouse." My son Bruno was there most or maybe all of the time. Bruno was a school friend of Raymond's son Thierry, and I remember overhearing arguments as to whose parent was more important. I was Raymond's boss at LAPP, but Raymond was my boss in the CNRS. I don't think they resolved the issue as to whether the Administrative Director or the Scientific Director of the school had more authority, but Bruno conceded the argument when Thierry pointed out that Raymond's wife Marie-France was his high-school teacher. Alain and Dominique were also in Les Houches at least some of the time, but for reasons I don't

Bruno and Mary K honoring Raymond at the close of the 1981 session on high energy physics of the Les Houches School.

remember, I had to commute back and forth on weekends to take care of things at home, so I didn't have much opportunity for Alpine hiking.

The Les Houches summer school was intended for advanced graduate students and beginning postdocs. We adhered strictly to that criterion, with two exceptions. One was Louis Witten, a well-known general relativist and the father of Ed Witten, a particle theory superstar, who became the first physicist to win the Fields Medal in mathematics. In the end Louis Witten did not attend, but the other exceptional applicant did attend, namely Izzy Singer, who in 2004 won the Abel Prize for mathematics together with Sir Michael Atiya for their 1962 joint work, which had an important impact on theoretical physics. Izzy was then in the Berkeley mathematics department and provided a counter-force to the Fermilab contingent, that included Chris Quigg, a Fermilab theorist and Les Houches lecturer, as well as Leon. Maybe the deciding factor was Izzy's daughter Melissa, with whom my son Bruno developed a brief flirtation during the school. In any case Bruno, who had been given the choice of moving to the US with me or staying with his father, opted definitively for Berkeley. Alain was already in college at the University of Washington, and Dominique was headed for the Santa Cruz campus of the University of California.

Discussing kaon physics with Murray Gell-Mann in 1972.

So not long after the school ended on September 11, Dominique, Bruno and I boarded a plane for San Francisco. Bruno Zumino had to take care of moving his belongings and relinquishing his apartment in the Geneva suburb of Petit Saconnex, and would join us in a month with our dog Couscous, whom my son Bruno wanted to keep with him.

Dave Jackson had finished his term as department chair in the summer of 1981, and went to CERN on sabbatical leave. He was still communicating with his Berkeley colleagues who were trying to arrange a senior staff position at LBL for Jean-Marc. When Dave learned from Bruno and myself, before we had decided between Berkeley and Fermilab, that my personal circumstances had changed, he called his successor, Leo Falicov, to tell him: "We're solving the wrong two-body problem." (Meanwhile Leon, who had already been apprised of the situation, was trying to arrange something for Bruno with the University of Chicago.) The Berkeley two-body problem was facilitated by a recent review of the department; the review committee, aware that there was already an offer out to me, had recommended hiring an additional senior, as well as a junior, particle theorist. Bruno was given a staff position at LBL for the first quarter, allowing time for a faculty meeting that led to his appointment to the faculty the following quarter.

Returning

We rented a car near the San Francisco airport and drove to a beach-side motel in Santa Cruz. We woke up to a gray, overcast day. Looking out at the fog hanging over Monterey Bay, Bruno said: "This is sunny California?" It was the first of many negative reactions my son had to his new environment. He experienced some culture shock at the El Cerrito High School he attended, and went back to France (accompanied by Couscous) after one year, but eventually returned to earn degrees in math and economics at UC Berkeley. After visiting the beautiful Santa Cruz campus and seeing Dominique settled in her residential college (although she moved out fairly soon and took a shared apartment downtown), Bruno and I drove to the house in Kensington, near Berkeley, that we were renting from a professor who was on sabbatical leave. He had canceled all his utilities and telephone accounts, and by the time we arrived there was no electricity. So Bruno and I went to a movie and came home to a dark house. It was no easy feat for me to open my own accounts, since I had no credit record. Getting a credit card was even harder. (I don't remember how I was able to rent the car without one, but we kept it for a very long time. We finally got around to buying our own car when we were going out of town and needed Dominique to chauffeur young Bruno; she was under 19 and could not drive a rental car.) Credit cards were not commonly used when I left the States in 1961, and did not become common in Europe until after I went back to the US, so I had never possessed one. During my time at Fermilab I had used a lab card for business travel. Dave Jackson lent me some dollars so I could open a bank account, in which my salary was deposited monthly, but when I applied for a credit card at the same bank, I was told they had "no way to verify" my salary. I wrote back that they were idiots, and they finally issued me a card with a credit limit of a few hundred dollars, which I quickly exceeded on travel to meetings, resulting in an immediate increase in the credit limit. By that time Bruno Zumino had sponsored me for an American Express card and a Macy's card, so I gradually started building up a credit record. Fortunately my offer from Berkeley included a university guaranteed mortgage at a 12% interest rate (as opposed to the then prevailing rate of about 18%), provided I buy a house by the end of 1982, which coincided with the date our landlord would reclaim his house. Maya Trilling, a realtor whose husband, George, was our colleague in the physics department, must have shown us about 100 houses. After getting over the price shock, we finally found a house we both liked — a private garden for me, and a view of the Golden Gate bridge for Bruno — just before the guaranteed mortgage was about to expire. There were two bids, which turned out to be identical, but the guaranteed loan won us the house.

The first day I arrived at the department, I went to meet the new chair, Leo Falicov, who informed me that I had to write him a letter accepting the position. It dawned on me that I had never formally applied for a job, except for summer jobs as a student, and never had to write a formal letter of acceptance. (In addition to Brookhaven, one summer I applied for a technical position with a company in Cleveland. Two men gave me a tour of the facility, took me to lunch, and, having never asked me a question about my technical abilities, joked about hiring me as some sort of receptionist. It was a pretty humiliating experience.)

I was generally very warmly accepted and respected by my physics colleagues at Berkeley, although the first faculty meeting was somewhat daunting. I walked into a room filled with about 60, mainly older, men. After a few opening remarks, the chair asked the assistant professors to leave; one person left. A bit later he asked the associate professors to leave, and one more person walked out. Since then the department has been considerably rejuvenated and diversified, at least gender-wise, if not ethnically.

But there were also some reality checks. As is customary I was free of teaching for the first quarter. The second quarter I was assigned quantum mechanics and that's when I learned that giving well-received lectures to physicists in my field was a far cry from teaching graduate students, especially teaching a course that non-physicists — with little appetite for the subject — were required to take. One day I was outside the classroom waiting for the professor who had given the previous lecture to leave, and I heard him ask my class: "How is she doing?" I saw a very embarrassed student looking at me, in a quandary about how to react. I've wondered since then if this was the same faculty member who, according to an LBL staff physicist, had said: "There will never be a woman on the physics faculty at Berkeley" a year or two before I arrived. I also remember him offering me a ride, along with a postdoc, up the hill from campus to the lab, just after I had received the E. O. Lawrence award from the Department of Energy. He announced to the postdoc that I had gotten this award, with what sounded to me like some disgruntlement. On another occasion, when I was visiting Fermilab in the early 1980s, probably for a committee meeting, there was a dinner with some important people, maybe members of the National Science Board or of the URA (Universities Research Association) Board of Trustees. Leon seated me at a table with some of these luminaries, thinking I would impress them by my scientific stature. They were of course all male, and many of them were not in academia; soon into the conversation it was clear that they assumed I was "somebody's" wife.

And there were, for a brief period during my first term of teaching, daily reports from Bruno Zumino about the graffiti in the men's bathroom on our office floor. It seems there was an argument about the new woman professor's looks. After a few days of this someone wrote PIGS! in protest, and then everything was cleaned off by the janitor and it ended there. I thought it was kind of amusing, and didn't take it very seriously. But perhaps I should have, given what I've learned since about male students' attitudes towards women that still apparently persist.

Dave Jackson, who is very meticulous and fair-minded, had set my salary at the same level as the three other theorists who were about my age. The difference was that two of them were childless and the other had just one child, and they had bought their homes in the late 1960s or early 1970s when both real estate prices and mortgage rates were a great deal lower than in 1982 when we bought our house. Berkeley could not match Bruno's CERN salary, but in order to even come close, he was offered an "above scale" salary, which meant it was not tied to a rank on the academic ladder. So his salary was initially about 50% more than mine, but our finances were separate. We shared common expenses, but took care of our own families, which in my case included expenses for Dominique and Bruno (Alain was supporting himself through work and student loans), with help from Jean-Marc. Fortunately, Dominique was automatically a resident of California by virtue of my membership in the UC Academic Senate, and public university tuition was still modest at the time. However my take-home salary barely covered my expenses. Berkeley had offered me a salary a bit higher than what I had from the CNRS, and, including the promised three months summer salary (three-ninths of my academic salary) it was slightly higher than the offer from Fermilab. (Due to budget cuts at LBL, the full three months was realized only once, and for most of my tenure it was two months.) At the time I came to Berkeley, I was so happy to be leaving Europe that it didn't occur to me to haggle over the salary, and it was not in my nature to engage in that sort of bargaining. On the other hand I had not anticipated the high cost of living in the Bay Area.

In addition, I was *"mieux sur le marché"*[16] with respect to my contemporaries in the department. Two of my female colleagues at other UC campuses told me my rank was too low; one said that my service on a 1983 High Energy Physics Advisory Panel (HEPAP) subpanel should have been sufficient to earn me a full-step promotion.[17] So at some point I went to Leo to complain and he recommended me for a meager half-step promotion.

Then sometime in the mid-1980s I got a call from Peter McIntyre of Texas A&M, whom I had met when he testified to our HEPAP subpanel in support of the SSC, which the Texans hoped would be built in their state. By then I was serving as the LBL theory group leader, a position that had previously been held, seemingly in perpetuity, by Geoff Chew (except

---

[16] "More valuable on the market," an expression used by Jacques Prentki when he had been instructed to nominate me as an alternate candidate for a French prize that was destined in advance to go to a male experimentalist.

[17] I later learned from serving on Ad Hoc promotion committees at Berkeley and other UC campuses, that the standards for promotion to any given rank were higher at UCB than elsewhere in the UC system.

for a semester in between, with Dave Jackson as acting group leader while I was on leave). Peter was offering me the position of Department Head. This is very different from a Department Chair, as at Berkeley, who has a limited term and governs with the consent of the faculty; the Head has an indefinite term and essentially runs the department. The idea was to recruit someone who could build up particle theory for the anticipated era of the SSC. I didn't have any desire to leave Berkeley, and my first instinct was to say "no thank you" and end the conversation. But I paused that thought and allowed myself to entertain the idea of moving. I was asked to suggest a salary and other perks I might want. I stayed mute on the salary (I knew it would be much better than my Berkeley salary, but had no idea as to what was an appropriate figure to suggest), but did offer the condition that my significant other would need a position. Peter was obviously embarrassed by his ignorance of the situation, and a day or two later I got a call from his consultant, Shelly Glashow, warmly encouraging us both to consider the move. So we took a trip to College Station. We were well treated and entertained, including a roadrunner sighting. Although I no longer had K-12 age children, I had expressed concern about efforts to introduce creationism in the Texas public schools. At the party they held for us they trotted out the department member who was active in the local chapter of the American Civil Liberties Union, as well as the one who had started the local public radio station that played classical music. (I remember one faculty member who showed us his home on a vast expanse of land that had been dirt cheap, extolling the benefits of his way of life. A couple of years later, I learned that the same person had moved to California.) In the end, John Reynolds, a meteorologist who was chairman of the Berkeley physics department at the time, and had little knowledge of particle physics, but had been informed that I had had something important to do with charm, managed to get me a raise of one-and-a-half or two steps to the rank that required "international recognition" and a new set of outside letters. Some of the letter writers told me that they wondered in their letters why I hadn't gotten that rank in the first place. So we stayed at Berkeley, and over the years I got promoted commensurately with my outside recognitions of achievement (prizes, election to scholarly academies). I had no more complaints about my situation at Berkeley. When I was serving on the Affirmative Action

Committee of the UCB Academic Senate, we did a comparative study of men's and women's salaries across several departments. The physics department, with a female contingent consisting at the time of myself and Marjorie Shapiro, who had joined us after Marjorie Olmstead left, was the only one where women came out ahead. This caused our chair to burst into laughter with the remark: "Mary K makes too much money!"

My Survival Mechanism

I am still smoking. I should not admit to it. I know it's bad for my health and no one should ever start. I've voted more than once for raising taxes on cigarettes in California. I no longer smoke in my own house. Of course I learned long ago to forgo smoking in classes, lectures and interviews, in airplanes, meetings and so on. In those circumstances I don't miss it, but I still become desperate for a cigarette when it's allowed. In my later life, I had gum surgery with the after-effect that I can become very uncomfortable if I don't clean my teeth immediately after a meal; this becomes an urgent need when I know it's possible, but I seem to be able to forget about it when I'm out to dinner somewhere, with maybe a whole opera afterward. Perhaps these reflexes account for my early ability to accept life as it was, including a second-class status, but somehow not forever. Maybe this adaptability was part of my survival mechanism.

I endured many subtle and less subtle small insults as a young aspiring scientist, and even as a more established one. When I had been at CERN a very short time, still a student, I was sitting in the cafeteria with a group of people, including the MIT theorist Herman Feshbach, who had co-authored a classic textbook that I still have on my shelf (and who later became active in promoting gender and ethnic diversity in the MIT physics department). I think that was when I was still working with Stanghellini. Feshbach asked me what I was doing, and when I explained that I was studying theory and that my husband was an experimentalist at CERN, his observation was that this was the wrong way around: normally men do theory, and women do experiment. I took this as an insult to both women and experimentalists. He was not the only person to make a comment of this sort.

An incident that has been deeply buried in the depths of my subconscious, and surfaced only as I was writing these pages, was an extremely offensive pornographic, handwritten (I should say drawn, since there were also offensive illustrations) note stuck in my CERN mailbox. I was so horrified and embarrassed by it that I tore it up and threw it away and never told a soul, and I never had a clue as to who did it. Years later, when gender issues had become something people actually were aware of, I had a close friend who dealt upfront with harassment. She was a technician at CERN working with a group of men who had filled the walls of their workplace with girlie posters. One evening my friend posted a pinup from *Playgirl* magazine. The next morning it was gone, along with all the other pinups.

Then there was the secretary effect, meaning that if you were a woman you were assumed to be someone who was supposed to help the men. I always had an open-door policy; anyone who wanted to discuss physics was welcome in my office. This resulted in people wandering into my office, after passing all the offices occupied by males, to ask me for directions or some other kind of help. On one such occasion, after I had graduated to a single office on the top floor of the CERN theory division, I was about to throw a book at the intruder until he said: "Didn't you use to be at Nevis?" It turned out to be Walter LeCroy, a Columbia graduate who had started a company that provided instrumentation for high energy physics experiments, and he somehow remembered me from my summer at Nevis Laboratory as a Columbia graduate student. I was so flattered that he recognized me from my much younger days that I forgave him, and we had a nice chat. Since the women on the CERN administrative staff were for the most part well dressed, wearing skirts and high heels, many of the women doing more technical work at some point started wearing pants to combat the secretary effect.

On another occasion I was an invited speaker at a conference in Southampton, England. I arrived the day before the conference began and attended a preconference reception. I was sitting around a table with a group of people, including the person who had written the letter of invitation to me, but whom I had never previously met. At some point he started a soliloquy ridiculing women in physics. Being used to these things, I didn't bother to argue with him; I was kind of amused. Later in the conversation, someone suggested that we introduce ourselves. When I said my name, the orator in question turned red-faced, and suddenly became very solicitous, asking me if I had had a comfortable trip.

In the early 1970s, our family twice spent a summer month or two at SLAC, where Jean-Marc was participating in an experiment with Mel Schwartz, and I was given a desk in the theory group. The women's lib movement was in the headlines, and Sidney Drell hosted a party at which he was complaining about feminist excesses, exemplified by bra burning (albeit conceding, to my mind somewhat secondarily, that women did have some cause for grievance). That was long before his daughter Persis had become an accomplished physicist herself (and as I often told people, responsible for me getting a job at UCB).

One of the most disturbing incidents occurred on a train to Hamburg, where I was traveling to give a talk promoting an electron–proton collider called CHEEP[18] that was a candidate for the next large CERN project. This was a brainchild of our friend Bjorn Wiik of DESY. John Ellis had originally been slated to give the talk, but he had a conflict so I went instead. The director of DESY, Volker Sörgel, was on the same train, and

With Nicola Cabibbo and Tini Veltman at DESY in 1977.

---

[18] I don't remember exactly what the acronym stood for — sometimes people stretch things to make the acronym come out the way they want. The machine was not built at CERN, but was resurrected as HERA (Hadron Electron Ring Accelerator) and built at DESY.

invited me to share a drink in his compartment. After a few pleasantries, he spent the remainder of my visit expounding on the fact that his wife, who had also studied physics, did the right thing by giving up her aspirations for a career to take care of her children. I found this incredible and especially offensive, since I was making the trip as a guest of his laboratory.

There were even close friends and supporters who had lapses of sexism. A prime example is Jacques Prentki, whom I have mentioned several times before. Another, less egregious, example is André Lagarrigue, the leader of the Gargamelle collaboration. He was on the "jury" (examination committee) for my own thesis, made complimentary remarks about my work, and was always very supportive. Yet when I served on a thesis jury for another woman, which he also chaired, he couldn't help but make a comment to the effect that "women are always very pedantic." I don't remember his exact words in French, but I was struck by the fact that he would make such a statement with another woman participating in the jury's deliberations.

My good friend Tini Veltman came into my office one day and gave me a long lecture about how I should be home taking care of my children instead of leaving them in the care of *au pair* girls. Many years later, his daughter Helene became my Ph.D. student at Berkeley. To add a touch of humor in a talk I gave in Tini's honor at the University of Michigan, I pointed this out; in other words, as my friend Leon remarked after my talk: "You not only took care of your own kids, you took care of his." In fact, before Helene was a graduate student, there had been a period when my husband Bruno and I were at Fermilab and Helene was there without her parents. The three of us went regularly to science fiction movies, so we had already become something of a family.

I basically reacted to all of these incidents as small nuisances; they had no real impact on my ability to function in my profession. What eventually became more than a nuisance was my situation at CERN. I don't remember exactly when my friend Carolyn Villain lent me her copy of Betty Friedan's *The Feminine Mystique*. It was eye-opening. Before then I had never questioned my second-class status at CERN; I just assumed that all the Fellows or junior staff members hired by CERN must be better than I. It took me many years to come to question that assumption.

Leon and Mary K at Les Houches.

Jacques Prentki celebrating a birthday.

My "survival mechanism" apparently kept me going all those years at CERN (even after reading Betty Friedan). But finally I found it imperative to move back to the US, in no small part for fear of becoming embittered if I stayed in Europe. I didn't want my personality to change for the worse.

Afterlife

Once I returned to the US I was immediately drafted onto numerous committees. I had barely arrived when I got a call from a representative of the CSWP (Committee on the Status of Women in Physics) of the American Physical Society (APS). They instructed me to join the APS and nominated me for a Fellowship before my department at Berkeley had time to get around to doing so. Then in 1983 I found myself serving on the CSWP, and two years later as its chair. The APS also set up a "blue ribbon" panel on Academic Positions for Women in Physics and Astronomy, which was supposed to enable the transfer of women physicists from industry and government laboratories to academia, where they would have a greater impact as role models. The only problem was that, except for the first meeting, the male members of the panel — who had the most clout — never showed up. I put one woman physicist in contact with a university that had a position open, but that's as far as it got. In the end the panel accomplished nothing and was disbanded.

In the spring after my arrival at Berkeley, I was appointed to a DOE survey of the university theoretical physics programs that they were funding. I was a member of a subpanel chaired by David Gross. David was an old friend from his days as a CERN summer visitor; after lunch we used to play what the French call "baby foot" (table soccer, at which I was hopeless). The panels met at Fermilab. After we had reviewed all the programs, we had a chat about general issues in our field. This resulted in the creation of a US summer school, in the model of Les Houches or the similar school in Cargèse, Corsica. There had been an analogous tradition

With Julius Wess and Bruno Zumino at the April 1988 meeting of the APS in Baltimore.

in the US at Brandeis, but for some reason that school had been discontinued. The Theoretical Advanced Study Institute in Elementary Particle Physics (TASI) began in 1983, originally changing locale every summer, but finally settling at the University of Colorado at Boulder. I served on its Advisory Board for five years. The other issue we tackled was an overhaul of the APS journal *Physical Review*, or at least the particle physics section of that journal, *Physical Review D* (PRD). At the time, the leading theorists were mostly publishing in the European journal *Nuclear Physics* for two reasons. First, the *Physical Review* charged a per page fee for publication, while *Nuclear Physics* did not.[19] Secondly, the standards for acceptance were much higher in *Nuclear Physics* than in the *Physical Review*. We enlisted the help of Lowell Brown, who was chairing another subpanel of the survey committee and for a long time served as an

---

[19] But they charged much higher fees to libraries to purchase it. For that reason there was recently a movement to boycott it. International agreements for "open access" to articles in our field are in progress, and in some cases already implemented.

editor of PRD, and in time our suggestions for eliminating page charges and tightening standards were implemented. I don't remember if it was before or after this effort that I was also appointed to the Editorial Board of *Physical Review D*.

I was also giving many talks and trying to continue research. I was still finishing work I had begun at CERN, including some with John Ellis and others. During my short tenure on the CERN SPS Advisory Committee we were discussing a project (called an antiproton accumulator) that would collect antiprotons for the purpose of observing proton–antiproton annihilation into charmonium states, allowing detailed studies of their decays. The experimentalists were worried about background from pions emitted with charmonium states. I think I remarked that one might learn something from these events because of the theorems that relate processes with low energy pion emission to pure charmonium production rates. That led to a collaboration with Luciano Maiani, my fellow theorist on the committee, and Roberto Petronzio; we showed that these events provided information on the quantum numbers of the charmonium states. I also co-authored papers with Berkeley colleagues and students on how to search for light supersymmetric partners of Standard Model particles. Then in the spring of 1983, I was invited to spend a semester at Fermilab, and Bruno at the University of Chicago. We were provided with a house on the Fermilab site, and Dan Friedan lent us his apartment in Hyde Park at minimal or no charge. Its furnishings consisted of a bed, a table, a couple of chairs, a state-of-the art sound system and a closet full of jeans. Dan was the son of Betty Friedan and had been a student of Izzy Singer at Berkeley (along with another of Izzy's students, the son of the renowned antifeminist Phyllis Schafly). He had left us signed checks to pay his bills, but at some point there was a small problem and, as per instructions, I called his mother to straighten it out. Bruno urged me to tell her how much I admired her, but she sounded very business-like on the phone, and I didn't have to the courage to intrude into her space.

We split our time between Fermilab and Chicago every week, except when I was away for meetings of the 1983 HEPAP Subpanel, informally known as the "Woods Hole Panel" because the final, week-long, meeting was traditionally held at the National Academy of Sciences (NAS)

Conference Center at Woods Hole, a research complex in Falmouth, Massachusetts. I had taken my student I-Hsui Lee with me to Fermilab (where she met her future husband Robert Shrock). We were able to complete our paper on K decays to photinos, the supersymmetric partners of photons, with my Berkeley colleague Mahiko Suzuki and his student, but I didn't accomplish much else in the way of research that semester. The panel had to visit every national high energy physics laboratory, and read letters from the entire high energy physics community. My desk at Fermilab became covered end-to-end with committee documents. There were two principle issues at stake. (1) Should we recommend construction of a proton–proton collider, with an energy of 20 trillion billion electron volts per proton, that had been studied in detail by a working group at a 1982 meeting in Snowmass, Colorado? (2) Should we recommend completion of the Colliding Beam Accelerator (CBA) at Brookhaven?

Physics at a Trillion Electron Volts

The CBA had been born in the early 1970s as "Isabelle," a proposed proton–proton collider with 200 billion electron volts of energy per proton. This energy was justified by something called the "unitarity limit." Unitarity is a mathematical formulation of the statement that the sum of probabilities of all possible outcomes of the collision of two particles (or of the decay of a single particle) is one. In particular, no single outcome can have a probability exceeding one. Isabelle had been conceived before the development of the Standard Model. At that time, the known weak interactions were well described by the Fermi theory that postulated a direct interaction among four fermions, but the theory was not mathematically consistent. In other words, because the weak coupling was small, you could successfully predict probabilities using the classical theory without worrying about corrections from multiple particle interactions. But if you tried to calculate these corrections, you would get an infinite result because you had to include all possible contributions, including those with very high energy particles being emitted and reabsorbed. These became larger as the energy increased. By the same token, if you calculated the fermion–fermion interaction rate using the classical theory, the probability for an interaction grew with energy, until at some point the collision probability exceeded unity; this is what is meant by the unitarity limit. It does not imply that the laws of probability will be violated, but rather that the theory becomes strongly interacting, and that some new physics must come into play to damp the growth of the interaction rate. The total of 400 billion electron volts of energy in the two colliding proton beams at Isabelle was meant to overreach this unitarity limit, which was generally taken to be 300 billion electron volts.[20] The project was recommended by HEPAP in 1974, and its construction began in 1978. However in 1981 the magnets did not perform as expected and a complete overhaul of the project was undertaken, including the name change to CBA in 1982, and an upgrade to 400 billion electron volts of energy per proton.

By the time our HEPAP subpanel met in the spring of 1983, many things had changed since the conception of Isabelle. The "new physics" required to damp the high energy growth of the Fermi theory interaction rate had already been identified: the direct four-fermion couplings were replaced by the exchange of W and Z bosons. This provided the needed damping at an energy determined by the W and Z masses of around 100 billion electron volts, well below the unitarity limit. These particles had not yet been produced, but the success of the theory in describing neutrino experiments, as well as neutral current effects in other processes, strongly supported the GWS electroweak theory. On June 6, during the (second, unplanned) final week of meetings of the HEPAP Subpanel, Carlo Rubbia pulled out a copy of the New York Times, with the headline "Europe 3, U.S. Not Even Z-Zero." The W and Z had been produced in the CERN proton–antiproton collider, with the predicted masses. The following year Carlo and Simon van der Meer were awarded the Nobel Prize for this discovery.

But now there was a new unitarity limit. The measured properties of Standard Model processes were consistent with the predictions of the electroweak theory that followed from the assumption of gauge

---

[20] As it happened, I attended a workshop on Isabelle at Brookhaven in 1973, where I wrote an internal note pointing out that, correctly calculated, the unitarity limit is actually two or three times higher (as had been found previously by, respectively, T. D. Lee in a 1971 Brookhaven study and I. Ya. Pomeranchuk in a Soviet journal in 1970) depending on the process considered.

transformations that leave the laws of nature invariant, but not the world in which we live, implying that the symmetry is spontaneously broken (see box on page 80). There was no direct evidence for the origin of symmetry breaking, or indeed for the very existence of a symmetry-breaking mechanism. The assumption of a Higgs field was the simplest possibility, but there were alternatives. Even in the simplest case, the mass of the Higgs particle H was not known. What was known was that this mass was proportional to the coupling constant that governed the strength of Higgs–Higgs interactions: the higher the mass, the stronger the coupling. As explained on pages 81 and 82, the Higgs particle originally had four components. In addition to the "real" Higgs scalar H, there are three other scalars, sometimes called $w^{\pm}$ and z, that become the "third" spin components of the $W^{\pm}$ and Z — the components with no spin projection along the boson direction of motion. If the H mass is very large, these components of the vector bosons, remembering their origin as w and z, have correspondingly large interaction rates. An infinite H mass is equivalent to no Higgs particle at all, in which case the theory makes no sense, and, just as in the Fermi theory, collision rates grow with energy, and the classical rate will exceed the unitarity limit at some point.

This second unitarity limit was first formulated in 1977 by Ben Lee, Chris Quigg and Hank Thacker, who showed that the W–W interaction rate will exceed the unitarity limit at some collision energy if the Higgs mass is 1 TeV or more.[21] Later, in 1984, Mike Chanowitz and I inverted their argument and showed that for an extremely large H mass (or no H at all) the unitarity limit was exceeded at a collision energy of 1.8 TeV.

Even if this unitarity limit is evaded by the simplest Standard Model Higgs mechanism, as seems to have turned out to be the case with the discovery, 29 years later, of a 125 GeV (0.125 TeV) scalar particle, which at the time of writing is consistent with the predicted properties of the Higgs particle, there was reason to expect that there would be additional new physics at, or not far above, the TeV energy scale. This reason is the "hierarchy problem" already alluded to in the context of supersymmetry: something is needed to cancel corrections from multiparticle interactions

---

[21] TeV is short for Tera electron volts, or a trillion electron volts.

to the value v of the Higgs field. Without such cancellations, it is hard to understand why v is not as large as the GUT energy or the Planck energy.

In addition to supersymmetry, candidate theories included "Technicolor," in which there are no elementary scalars. Instead the eaten scalars that form the extra components of the W and Z are bound states of elementary fermions ("techniquarks"). In its original form, as proposed independently in 1979 by Steve Weinberg and Lenny Susskind, this was an elegant idea; however it generated masses only for the vector bosons. It became much less attractive when it was extended to allow for fermion masses without at the same time generating large neutral current flavor violation, which was not observed, and it is by now strongly constrained by precise measurements of the W and Z properties. Another proposal, "compositeness," postulates that quarks themselves are bound states of yet more elementary fermions; this is helpful for the gauge hierarchy problem only if these new particles are confined within quarks and leptons inside a radius of the order of an inverse TeV (about a thousandth of a trillionth of a centimeter), which is all but ruled out by now. This left supersymmetry as the leading candidate among the early contenders for new physics at the TeV energy scale. More recently, different scenarios have emerged in which there are extra spatial dimensions that are much larger than the Planck length of a billionth of a trillionth of a trillionth of a centimeter: inverse TeV scale dimensions or even infinitely large dimensions. In these scenarios there is no hierarchy problem: the energy where gravity becomes strong is much lower than the observed Planck energy of two thousand trillion TeV, but gravitational interactions appear Planck-scale suppressed to us because most of the gravitons — the mediators of the gravitational interactions — "leak" into the extra dimensions, and we don't feel their effects.[22]

An exploration of the TeV energy range would require colliding proton beams with many TeVs of energy in each beam. This is because one needed TeV-energy collisions among the *partons* inside the proton.

There were — and still are — other unresolved issues in the Standard Model. For, example, there is no understanding of the pattern of fermion masses, ranging from the (nearly) massless neutrinos and the electron mass of a half a million electron volts, one eighteen hundredth of the

---

[22] See for example *Warped Passages* by Lisa Randall (Ecco/HarperCollins, 2005).

A proton at rest can roughly be thought of as three quarks at rest, with most of its mass arising from the energy in the color field that binds the quarks together. When the proton is accelerated, so are the quarks inside it. An accelerating electron emits photons, predominantly along its direction of motion; the photons can in turn convert to electron–positron pairs, resulting in an electromagnetic "shower." These emissions increase as the energy of the electron increases. In the same way, an accelerating quark emits gluons that in turn create quark–antiquark pairs, more so as the energy increases. This means that a particle probing the partons inside the proton can interact with gluons and antiquarks as well as with quarks. In fact the first experiments with sufficient collision energy (a couple of GeV*) to reveal the presence of partons showed that about half the proton energy was carried by gluons. The electron and neutrino probes used in those experiments did not interact directly with the gluons, but the quarks and antiquarks that they did interact with accounted for only half of the proton energy. The antiquarks accounted for about 5%, leaving at most one sixth of the proton energy for each of the original three quarks of the proton at rest. It was expected that for parton collision energies in the* TeV *range, this would be reduced to about a tenth, and that the contribution of antiquarks would be considerably higher. The good news was that proton–proton colliders, which were easier to build with a high rate of collisions, would be competitive with proton–antiproton colliders for observing interactions that required quark–antiquark annihilation. The bad news was that in order to explore parton collisions of several* TeV *in energy, one needed a proton collision energy of several tens of* TeV.

proton mass, to the top quark mass of about 175 GeV, almost 180 times the proton mass. There were ideas about how new symmetries might account for this pattern of masses, but no guidelines as to the energy scale at which they might become manifest. In contrast, the unitarity limit associated with spontaneous breaking of the electroweak gauge symmetry, and the related hierarchy problem, provided a clear signpost for new physics in the TeV energy range that the vast majority of the high energy physics community recognized.

There were however a few skeptics, within the HEPAP subpanel and in the general community. This skepticism inspired me to enlist Mike Chanowitz to undertake with me a serious analysis of what scattering among *W* and *Z* bosons might look like if there were no elementary Higgs particle with a mass less than a TeV. While we were starting on this project, Sally Dawson and Bob Cahn had calculated the rate for *H* production in proton–proton collisions by a mechanism,[23] now known as *W* fusion, in which each proton emits a *W* and the two *W*s "fuse" (or annihilate with one another) to form a Higgs boson. They were at the blackboard puzzling as to why the rate they found was so large. The accelerated quarks inside the protons emit left- and right-spinning *W*s and *Z*s much as they emit photons or gluons. These couple to the *H* with the usual weak coupling constant g_w, suggesting a lower rate than what was found. Like the *H*, the *w* and *z* have couplings to quarks suppressed by a factor of the quark mass divided by the Higgs field value: $g_q = m_q/v$, so they were not expected to contribute significantly to the *W* fusion process: the light quarks have masses almost a hundred thousand times smaller than the Higgs field value *v*. However, it was precisely the emission of these "third" components of the vector bosons that Mike and I were using to study their strong rescattering rates. It turns out that their couplings are identical to the eaten Higgs couplings (a fact first noted in 1974 by John Cornwall, David Levin and George Tiktopoulos) up to corrections of order m_w/E_w, where m_w is the *W* mass and E_w is its energy. This correction is suppressed in the high energy limit we were interested in *except* in *W* or *Z* emission from a light particle, where it is enhanced by a compensating factor E_w/m_w (and is not proportional to the quark mass). What Bob and Sally were finding was the contribution of the *H* coupling to *w* and *z*, which grows with the Higgs mass.

Mike and I also used the fact that in the large mass limit for the "real" Higgs *H*, the "eaten" Higgs particles *w* and *z* behave exactly like the pions of QCD with an appropriate adjustment of the energy scale at which strong scattering occurs, because their couplings have the same flavor and chiral symmetries as the pions; Technicolor, mentioned above, is one explicit realization of such a scenario. This allowed us to make definite statements about *W* and *Z* interactions in the TeV energy region. We showed that signals of new physics would be visible at the SSC even in the absence of a Higgs particle *H* with a mass low enough for its discovery, and conversely that the absence of any new physics signal would imply that a lighter

---

[23] The analogous process for Higgs production in e^+e^- annihilation had been calculated in 1979 by Tim Jones and Serguey Petcov.

Higgs *H* had been missed and should be looked for more diligently. Mike called this a "no-lose" scenario, and our results prompted Savas Dimopoulos to remark in a Berkeley Colloquium that we had proved "a very important theorem," namely that "the SSC is not waste of money."

The more contentious issue facing the 1983 HEPAP Subpanel was the fate of the CBA. The DOE was strongly committed to its completion. We were told that there would be sufficient financial and human resources to complete the CBA and construct the (as yet unnamed) SSC in a timely fashion. Given our marching orders, as one tormented Subpanel member put it, the CBA had to be "positively evil" for us to stop it from going forward.

However, the majority of the high energy physics community felt that it was too little too late, and would drain resources from the 40 TeV collider as well as the other elements of the program that were well underway. The Tevatron, a proton–antiproton collider being built at Fermilab, would come in with a much higher energy (one TeV per beam), albeit with a considerably lower interaction rate, than the CBA. On the other hand there was strong pressure from the DOE, as well as from senior members of the East Coast particle physics establishment, to proceed with construction of the CBA. They could not envision giving up the idea of Brookhaven as the center of US high energy physics. Even some of us who were firmly convinced that going forward with the CBA would be a mistake (as it would have been, given what we know now) had sentimental ties to Brookhaven, as the place where our early careers had been nurtured. In addition, the European establishment was counting on the CBA to provide "spigots" for their physicists to have something to do while awaiting the construction of their own high energy collider that was to become the LHC. Carlo Rubbia, one of the two CERN physicists on the Subpanel, was an interesting case. A brilliant physicist, he was acutely aware of the physics potential of the SSC, and the enthusiasm among the younger members of the high energy physics community for the SSC and the lack thereof for the CBA. He freely acknowledged this at dinners with his fellow panelists, but wore a distinctly CERN hat during our meetings.

The meetings at Woods Hole (that were to have led to our final recommendations) were tense and exhausting. One day when we had concluded an after-dinner session, I was relaxing with a beer and enjoying

Wood's Hole 1983: HEPAP (Wojcicki) sub-panel in session. Around the table, from 7 p.m., Earle Fowler (in red), Carlo Rubbia, Bruce Winstein, Lee Pondrom, Tom Appelquist, Jack Vandervelde and Maury Tigner (both hidden), Denis Keefe, Stan Wojcicki, Frank Sciulli, John Adams, Brig Williams, Mary Gaillard, Sam Treiman, Charlie Baltay, ?? (back of head).

Also John Rees (hidden) between Sciulli and Adams, and Art Kernan (back of head). Photo by Dave Jackson.

the view. Jim Leiss, the DOE Associate Director for High Energy and Nuclear Physics, and his deputy for high energy physics, Bill Wallemeyer, joined me. Jim immediately started pressuring me to support the CBA. I became angry and asked him why they had appointed a committee if they already knew the answer they wanted. Bill made him back off, and they left me alone. Years later Bill told me that we had made the right decision. But it was not without a struggle. After the final vote, we were told that we had to reconvene and try again. We were to meet at a later date at my old stomping ground, Nevis Laboratory.

In the interim I went back to Fermilab, where one of my colleagues, who had served on a HEPAP Subpanel the year before, said simply: "You got the wrong answer," when he learned that we had to meet again. Some members of that earlier panel thought that they had imposed sufficient conditions on the completion of the CBA that they had effectively killed it. But it did not die that easily. It was during this break between meetings that the Shelter Island Conference took place, with the press and interested parties providing additional pressure on the theorists from the Subpanel in attendance. There was one incident when a senior East Coast physicist started lecturing me on the virtues of the CBA, and Bruno, an old friend of his, deftly changed the subject and freed me from the onslaught. Bruno was well aware of the pressure I was under. He claimed that I kicked him in my sleep during that period, probably dreaming about Jim Leiss. Bruno and I had driven to Fermilab from Berkeley and had planned to drive back. But we would not have time to make the car trip home after my Nevis meeting. Bruno did not want to drive by himself, so when I left for Nevis he put the car on a train and flew home, carrying a tumbleweed that I had picked up on our trip out, and had carefully preserved. (Some years later a Japanese family renting our house during a sabbatical leave got rid of it; they didn't know about the "tumbling tumbleweeds" of my childhood.)

The meeting at Nevis was equally trying, except that I stayed at the home of Charlie Baltay. He and his family had been our neighbors for a year in France, and we had become good friends. There was one after-dinner meeting where the pro-CBA contingent made an effort to negotiate by bits and pieces with the "no on CBA" people, until I just said: "Stop!" We had come to a majority decision and they were simply trying to undo it by offering us "nickles and dimes," in the words of one sympathetic panel member from the pro-CBA group. In the end, after many votes and revotes, we reached the same conclusion as we had before, and the CBA was terminated. Besides writing a (contentious and divided) report, on the last day of our meeting we had to come up with a name for the 40 TeV collider. While many of us were scratching our heads to find a suitable and pronounceable acronym, Dave Jackson announced that he didn't want a pronounceable acronym and suggested the Superconducting Super Collider, or SSC, which it became.

There followed a flurry of activity in support of the SSC. There was a workshop at Berkeley, organized by Ian Hinchliffe, my colleague on the Subpanel Tom Appelquist and myself, and then a workshop in Chicago. I was asked by our Subpanel chair, Stan Wojcicki, to give a three-hour lecture series at a meeting of the American Association of Physics Teachers. A summary of my lectures was included in the book *Appraising the Ring* (URA 1988), a collection of articles about the SSC edited by Leon Lederman and Chris Quigg. Dave Jackson, Tom Appelquist and I wrote an article for the American Scientist on the virtues of the SSC, as

I did for the McGraw-Hill Yearbook of Science. My last effort was at a meeting for high school students in Washington, DC, called "Star SSC." My Berkeley colleagues, Bob Cahn and Mike Barnett, with whom I had traipsed the halls of Congress to promote the SSC, asked me to help them find a prominent woman to speak at this event. After my old friend Shirley Jackson declined because she was to meet with the French President François Mitterand in Paris that day, I was drafted. So I took a one-day trip to Washington, had a five-minute cameo appearance, and was gratified by the students who thanked me for trying to assure their future. One asked me to sign his T-shirt. But the SSC was not to be. Its cancellation in 1993 was devastating to the high energy physics community. At that time I was a member of HEPAP. There was a meeting in which an elder statesman of our community said that he felt that he had lost a child, an experience which he had actually endured.

I had also called Sharon Begley, the science editor of Newsweek, whom I had previously encountered at a meeting among women science journalists and UCB women scientists. She told me she might write something about young people losing their future, but she never did. The SSC cancellation did take its toll on young scientists and on the health of our field in the US. I had a very brilliant student who had done sufficient research for his Ph.D. thesis and had even started writing it. But he was already depressed by the difficulty his fellow students had in finding jobs (and by the loss by the San Francisco Giants to the Oakland As in the 1989 Battle of the Bay). The cancellation of the SSC was the final straw, and he simply dropped out of sight. Another student of mine had gotten a postdoctoral appointment on an SSC fellowship; these were Texas-financed fellowships for which I had been asked to serve on the next selection committee. The fellowships evaporated. My student's employers managed to find him money for a year, and he got another postdoc the following year, but a few years later left the field "because he had given all that he could to it." I don't know if the SSC cancellation played a role in that decision.

Two very close friends of mine who were working at the SSC decided to leave the field and get jobs in the private sector so that they could stay on their ranch in Texas. I'm not sure how many others left the field, but

I even toyed with the idea of giving up research and putting more effort into public education on the value of basic research, expanding our understanding of the universe we live in, and just plain intellectual curiosity. Maybe that's why I accepted an appointment to the National Science Board (NSB). The first task force the Chair Dick Zare assigned me to was on setting priorities in government funding of science. The second, which I chaired, was on improving K-12 STEM (Science, Technology, Engineering and Math) education. One of our major recommendations was for a standardized curriculum, to take into account our mobile population, and to provide an incentive for textbook writers to emphasize depth over breadth (needed to cover all the different curricula that were in place). This idea seems to have gained some traction recently.

In the spring of my second year on the NSB, Bruno and I had planned a sabbatical leave in Paris and in Cambridge, England. That was when the Board would consider NSF funding for the US participation in the LHC, which by then was an approved project in Europe. The parameters for the LHC were limited by the dimensions of the LEP tunnel at CERN, in which it was to be built. Its target energy, with 7 TeV of energy per proton, was well below that of the SSC. It was argued that this would be compensated for by the much higher projected interaction rate, which would allow for the detection of the rare collisions when the partons have a substantial fraction of the proton energy. This high collision rate in itself presented a challenge for experimentalists, who had to devise detectors that could sort out the interesting events from multiple boring ones which would appear in their detectors at the same time. Dick Zare, who was a strong supporter of this collaboration, which represented the only remaining opportunity for US physicists to participate in research at the high energy frontier, insisted that I come back from my sabbatical for that meeting to lead the questioning of my old friend Chris Llewellyn-Smith, who by then had become the CERN Director General. So I took a bus from Cambridge to Heathrow and boarded a plane to Washington carrying only a laptop case, containing my grown-up clothes for meetings and my toiletries; this astonished the US customs agent, but he didn't give me any trouble. I grilled Chris with the appropriate questions, which he answered deftly, and NSF support for the LHC was approved.

In Antarctica as an NSB member.

The original target date for the SSC had been 1993, the very year that it was canceled. Experimental exploration of the TeV region would be put off for another decade. Perhaps that is also why my physics interests gravitated to an energy scale even more inaccessible to experimental exploration, namely the Planck energy of two thousand trillion trillion electron volts, or two thousand trillion TeV.

Physics at the Planck Energy

At the same time that I was working with Mike Chanowitz on strong W and Z interactions, Pierre Binétruy and I had started studying early universe physics in supersymmetric theories; this naturally led us to consider string theory, which had emerged as the leading contender for a finite theory of gravity and for the unification of the four fundamental forces of nature that I had first learned about from Bob Adair in 1959 as a summer student at Brookhaven.

String theory replaces the ("zero dimensional") point-like particles of field theory with (tiny) one-dimensional objects that can be segments of a curve ("open strings") or deformations of a circle ("closed strings"). It was first introduced into particle physics as a candidate theory of strong interactions. However, as originally formulated, string theory only made sense in 26 space-time dimensions, which means that in addition to a single time dimension, there had to be 25 spatial dimensions, as opposed to our observed three. Then the supersymmetric version of string theory, called superstring theory, was developed; it required only 10 space-time dimensions — time plus nine spatial dimensions. In string theory, what we observe as particles are the vibrational modes of oscillating strings, much like the harmonics of a violin string. The massless particles are the lowest modes; higher modes have masses that are integer multiples of the string tension — the effort it takes to stretch the string. In particle physicists' units ($c = \hbar = 1$ with c the speed of light and $\hbar$ Planck's constant), the string tension can be expressed as an area, or in units of the inverse of energy squared. In the original application to strong interactions, the tension was taken to be about a half of an inverse squared GeV, or roughly a hundredth of the squared range of strong interactions, which is about a tenth of a trillionth of a centimeter. However, in addition to the troublesome extra dimensions, string theory required a massless spin-two particle, and there was no such particle observed among the lightest hadrons. But this made string theory an ideal candidate for a theory of gravity, which demands such a particle: the graviton h (see table on page 41) must have two units of spin in order to correctly describe the observed properties of gravitational interactions. In the string theory for gravity, the string tension is of the order of the square of the Planck length (a billionth of a trillionth of a trillionth of a centimeter) or the inverse square of the Planck energy (two thousand trillion trillion electron volts).[24]

It turns out that supersymmetry is necessary for the full consistency of string theory, which therefore lives in 10 dimensions. To make contact with what we observe, six of the nine spatial dimensions have to curl up with radii so small that we do not notice them.

Take a sheet of paper, which is a two-dimensional surface. Roll it up to form a cylinder. A probe that cannot resolve distances smaller than the diameter of the cylinder will see only the dimension along its length. A vector on the sheet of paper has two possible orientations: along its length or its width. The component pointing in the direction that gets rolled up appears as a dot in the one-dimensional flat space along the side of the cylinder. A vector particle in the 10-dimensional space-time of superstring theory will appear as a vector plus six scalars in the four dimensional space-time that we observe.

---

[24] At least as originally formulated. Subsequently scenarios were proposed with a much lower string (and therefore gravitational) energy scale, as well as much larger hidden dimensions than the scenario discussed below. (See *Warped Passages* by Lisa Randall.)

However, supersymmetry is a necessary, but not sufficient, condition for consistency of the theory. Any superstring theory that might resemble the universe that we observe is a 10-dimensional theory of supergravity coupled to gauge bosons and their fermionic supersymmetry partners. Such theories generally have multiple interactions that couple six bosons to one another, analogous to the triple boson couplings of four-dimensional gauge field theories that would spoil gauge invariance if they were present. In the 10-dimensional case these couplings include gravitons as well as vector bosons, and can break rotational invariance — which as far as we know is an exact symmetry of nature — as well as gauge invariance.

In 1984, Mike Green and John Schwarz showed that these unwanted couplings could be avoided for two specific gauge theories, both with 496 independent gauge transformations, of which 16 are just multiplicative operations that form an Abelian subset (see box on pages 57–58). One of these string theories, in which the gauge transformations are just rotations in a 32-dimensional abstract space (similar to isospin rotations in a three-dimensional abstract space — or to ordinary rotations in ordinary space), had already been formulated. The other one, found after the Green–Schwarz result by David Gross, Jeff Harvey, Emil Martinec and Ryan Rohm (GHMR), seemed particularly promising for the unification of the four forces because it potentially contains the particle content of the Standard Model.

What determines the properties of the low energy theory is the way in which the six hidden dimensions curl up. For example, if you take the piece of paper you already rolled up, according to the instruction in the above box, and bend it around to put the two ends of the cylinder together, you get a torus (shaped like a doughnut). But geometrically, you haven't done anything. You started with a flat surface, and it is still flat. If you start out with six dimensions, you can make three tori, but you still haven't done anything to change the geometry of your space. This means that all the particles that existed in your 10-dimensional world will still exist in your four-dimensional one. So will all the symmetry.

One way to see if a space is flat is to move a vector around the space, keeping it oriented on a plane tangent to the space at every point along the trajectory, without rotating it in that plane. If it always comes back to its starting point oriented the same way as it started out, no matter what path it took, the space is flat. This is the case for a vector moving on a sheet of paper, and nothing changes if the paper is smoothly deformed into a cylinder or a torus. But it's not true on the surface of a sphere. If you start at the North Pole and move a vector in the direction of its orientation, by the time you get to the Equator it will be pointing due south. It continues to point south as you move it along the equator by 180°. If you then move it back to the North Pole it will get there with an orientation in the opposite direction from the one it started out with. The full set of transformations on the vector that can be performed by taking it along different paths on a sphere is just the set of rotations in a plane tangent to the surface of the sphere; the vector can rotate by any angle α (alpha) from zero to 2π. The components of vector particles that are not invariant under trips around the hidden six dimensions do not appear in our low energy four-dimensional world because they cannot be uniquely defined: their orientation in the hidden space is not fixed.

Fermions also change their orientation as they move around on a curved space. So can supersymmetry operators; they behave like fermions. A single supersymmetry in four-dimensional space-time has two

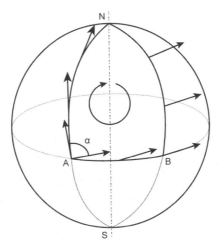

A vector moves from point A on the Equator to the North Pole N, then from N to point B, and finally from B to A, without changing its direction in the plane tangent to the surface of the sphere at each point along its trajectory. It arrives back at point A rotated by an angle α (alpha). Figure from Wikipedia.

operations: raising and lowering spin by half a unit; it has the properties of a spin-$\frac{1}{2}$ fermion.

A vector in n spatial directions has n orientations; it can point in any of the n different directions in that space. A fermion in a higher dimensional space also has more possible orientations than in four dimensions, and so does a supersymmetry operator. In 10 dimensions there are four spin-raising and four spin-lowering supersymmetry operations. If the six hidden dimensions remained flat, for example, by being paired into three tori, all these operations would remain symmetries of the four-dimensional world, which would have four supersymmetries, a situation that we know cannot encompass the Standard Model. On the other hand, if the hidden dimensions formed a six-dimensional sphere, there would be no supersymmetry left in four dimensions because all of the supersymmetry operators would undergo the full set of rotations in six dimensions as they move around the surface of the sphere. Philip Candelas, Gary Horowitz, Andy Strominger and Ed Witten used a six-dimensional space, discovered by the mathematician Eugenio Calabi and studied by Shing-Tung Yau, which has the property that just one spin-raising operator (and its spin-lowering counterpart) remain unchanged as they travel around in the hidden space. This leaves just one supersymmetry in four dimensions.

The gauge symmetry in the GHMR theory consists of two identical sets of gauge transformations, called[25] "E_8" — one assumed to describe our world, with the other describing a "hidden" world of the four-dimensional theory. The two worlds know about each other only through gravitational interactions.

An E_8 theory has too much symmetry to allow for a realistic description of our world. However curvature of the hidden space arises from non-vanishing gravitational fields; these fields are related by supersymmetry to fermion fields. The fermion fields must all vanish in order to preserve invariance under rotations in our three-dimensional space. This can be achieved while preserving supersymmetry by turning

---

[25] The E stands for "exceptional," meaning that this is not part of a general class, such as rotations in n dimensions (orthogonal groups) or transformations on complex vectors in n dimensions (unitary groups), and 8 is the number of multiplicative operations.

on some vector fields with their spins oriented along some direction in the hidden space, which breaks the gauge symmetry down to one of the sets of transformations that had already had been found suitable for a GUT that unifies the strong and electroweak interactions of the Standard Model.

Yet there is still a problem of too much symmetry. The small mass particles that populate the world we observe are remnants of the gauge bosons and their fermion counterparts in the 10-dimensional theory. These must remain unchanged under the *combined* effects of traveling around the curved hidden space and around the gauge fields that have non-vanishing values.

Scalars — with no spins to rotate — appear in the low energy four-dimensional theory if they are invariant under the broken symmetry transformations. However there is just one scalar particle in the 10-dimensional theory. This scalar is called the "dilaton" and has no gauge couplings at all. Instead the value of the associated field determines the strength of the gauge couplings at the string energy scale. The other scalars in the four-dimensional theory come from some of the vector particles that are not invariant under the broken symmetry and whose spins point in some direction in the hidden six-dimensional space. One of these will appear in four dimensions if its change due to curvature exactly cancels the effect of its gauge couplings when it makes a trip around a closed path on the curved space.

In the E_8 theory, this turns out to give scalars in the four-dimensional theory with the same quantum numbers as all the Standard Model fermions, as well as the Higgs scalars needed for the supersymmetric extension of the Standard Model. Since this four-dimensional theory still has one supersymmetry, we get all the fermions of the Standard Model as well. However there is no scalar field with the right properties to break the residual GUT symmetry down to the Standard Model gauge symmetry by acquiring a very large value, as was the case, for example, in the Georgi–Glashow model discussed previously.

Fortunately, the curvature of the six extra dimensions provides a new, more elegant, way to accomplish this additional symmetry breaking. A non-vanishing gauge field can wind around a "hole" or a "tube" in the hidden space: this has the same effect as a Higgs field with the same gauge quantum numbers as the gauge field that gets turned on, which is what is

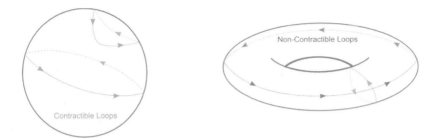

Every closed path on a sphere can be continuously shrunk down to a point. There are two types of closed paths on a torus that cannot be shrunk to a point: a path around the doughnut hole and a path that circles the doughnut by going through the hole. These paths are called "non-contractible loops." A gauge field can flow around a non-contractible loop in the hidden space of compactified 10-dimensional supergravity that is the large tension limit of superstring theory. Figure from Scienceforall.

needed to break the GUT down to something more closely resembling the Standard Model. Even though there is no longer a Grand Unified Theory in four dimensions, there is still coupling constant unification at the string energy scale, because the gauge couplings are all determined at that energy by the value of a single scalar field: the dilaton field of the 10-dimensional theory.

What I have described here is just one possibility out of many in the general context of string theory. There are altogether five string theories, and each of these allows for many possible universes. That is, there are many ways in which the six extra dimensions can curl up to give different gauge theories with different matter particles — and even different numbers of flat dimensions, like the ones we live in. This situation distressed many theorists until the "second string revolution," when it was realized that the five string theories are related to one another. A theory that has strong interactions can be turned into a different one with weak interactions by inverting the value of the coupling strength $\alpha = g^2/4\pi$. Or one that has a dimension curled up into a circle can be turned into another by inverting the radius of the circle. It was also discovered that all five theories can be obtained from something called "M-theory," that lives in 11 dimensions, by shrinking the eleventh dimension in one way or another. I'm not sure, and maybe nobody else is, what the "M" stands for.

The Mother of all theories? (There's an even more nebulous theory called F-theory — Father? — that lives in 12 dimensions.) Not a whole lot is known about M-theory except that it involves membranes, which are two-dimensional objects (as opposed to one-dimensional strings and the "zero" dimensional points of ordinary field theory). Still a different limit of M-theory gives a supergravity field theory in 11 dimensions; when seven of these dimensions are shrunk to points, one gets the $N = 8$ supergravity theory in four dimensions that my collaborators and I had worked on earlier, and which is still a subject of active research.

Many theorists were delighted by the discovery that the string theories could be united into a single theory. But there was still the problem of finding the right state of nature; in other words, how did we end up in the world we live in? Not only are there five different string theories (as well as many other points in the M-theory "landscape" — a term introduced by Raphael Bousso and Joe Polchinski), each string theory allows many different outcomes, depending on the size and shape of the hidden space. There has been a lot of activity in trying to count the number of possibilities in one of the string theories; this number was found to be very large — so large that it can in practice be thought of as infinite. At that point I think the theoretical community divided into two camps. One camp takes a probabilistic and anthropic approach: we should be living at a point in the landscape with the features that are the most probable within the subset of universes that are capable of supporting people (or some kind of entities) who are around to observe it.

The other group tries to find a specific solution that reproduces what we observe, and postpones worrying about how we got here. This camp (myself included) focuses mostly (but not exclusively) on the E_8 heterotic string theory or something close to it. My own efforts, in collaboration with Pierre Binétruy, Tom Taylor and my students and former students at Berkeley, have largely centered on supersymmetry breaking in this theory.

If supersymmetry provides a correct description of nature, we live in a world of broken supersymmetry, because we have not observed the supersymmetric partners of the known particles. There are two ways to break supersymmetry while preserving its ability to provide a technical solution to the "gauge hierarchy" problem. The first is "spontaneous" symmetry breaking (see box on page 80). The second is to introduce a few things into the theory that break supersymmetry, but are otherwise harmless. These include masses of scalar particles and their mixings with one another, masses of the fermion partners of gauge bosons, and couplings of three scalars to one another. Here "mixing" means that the scalars with well-defined flavor quantum numbers are not those with well-defined masses; the latter are admixtures of the former. This route leads to a large number of arbitrary parameters that have to be introduced into the theory. The more attractive route, namely spontaneous symmetry breaking, has been shown to be impossible in supersymmetric extensions of the Standard Model. For example it inevitability leads to the existence of at least one quark scalar superpartner that is lighter than all the quarks, as first shown by Savas Dimopoulos and Howard Georgi, and this is in direct contradiction with experiment.

For this reason it was proposed that there might be a "hidden" world in which supersymmetry is broken, and that the information of this is transmitted to our world only by gravitational interactions. The GHMR heterotic string provides this hidden world with the second E_8 (or whatever it becomes after symmetry breaking by trapped gauge fields around holes or tubes in the hidden space.) Supersymmetry can be spontaneously broken in the hidden world by strong interaction effects of the gauge couplings in that world. This is what I have been studying with my many collaborators. Results from the LHC have already severely constrained the set of parameters that determine the masses of superpartners for supersymmetry in general, and for this scenario in particular. We are all hoping for some sign of new physics to emerge.

There are other indications of new physics that do not rely on very high energy accelerator or collider experiments. For many years experiments led by Ray Davis observed a deficit of electron neutrinos arriving from the sun, compared with the predictions by John Bahcall and his collaborators. This suggested that neutrinos have very small masses, and that a neutrino with one flavor can turn into one of another flavor. This result was basically ignored by many theorists (including myself) for years as probably being due to a flaw in our understanding of the nuclear physics of the sun. But eventually Bahcall's model of the sun was independently confirmed, and experiments using reactors in Japan, as well as studies of neutrinos originating in the earth's atmosphere, confirmed that the neutrinos do indeed have masses and that they turn into one another as they travel along. The origin of these effects are as yet unknown and are a subject of active research.

We have also known for a long time of the existence of what's called "dark matter" in the universe. This is matter that is not visible because it interacts very weakly with ordinary matter and radiation; so far it has been detected only through its gravitational effects. The speed of an object in a stable orbit about a more massive object depends on the strength of the gravitational field it experiences. The earliest evidence for dark matter was the observation of orbital speeds that were larger than could be accounted for by the visible mass. This effect was first observed in the orbital velocities of stars in the Milky Way by Jan Oort in 1932, and in the orbital velocities of galaxies in clusters by Fritz Zwicky in 1933. Then in 1970 Vera Rubin established the same effect in the rotational speeds of galaxies. Some theorists proposed modifications to the Newton–Einstein theory of gravity to explain these results, but for most of the cosmology community the existence of dark matter was confirmed by the observation of the "Bullet Cluster" in 2004. This refers to the collision of two clusters of galaxies, resulting in the dispersion of ordinary matter by Standard Model interactions, whereas the dark matter in the clusters passed through essentially unaffected. The dark matter could be observed by "gravitational lensing," the bending of light as it passes around a massive object.

Dark matter has a natural home in supersymmetric theories. In the Standard Model the proton is stable. Given the particle content of the theory, gauge invariance, together with rotational invariance, assures that there is no coupling that can lead to proton decay. But in the supersymmetric extension of the Standard Model, with scalar particles that have the same flavor and color quantum numbers as the quarks and leptons, more couplings are allowed. If one includes all the couplings allowed by supersymmetry, gauge invariance and rotational invariance, one finds that the proton should decay very quickly. This can be avoided by introducing a new conserved quantum number[26] called "R-parity." All the particles of

---

[26] The ever more stringent limits being set on the lifetime of the proton suggest that an even stronger symmetry is needed; I showed in one of my papers that such a symmetry could arise as a remnant of the symmetries of the GHMR theory.

the Standard Model have positive R-parity, and all their superpartners have negative R-parity. As a consequence of R-parity, the supersymmetric partners can only be produced in pairs, and the lightest one should be stable. This makes supersymmetry a natural candidate for dark matter. During the expansion of the early universe, when the energy of the particles in the cooling plasma fell below that needed for ordinary particles to produce their supersymmetric partners, the latter decayed or annihilated into lighter particles. When their annihilation rate fell below the expansion rate of the universe, they simply decayed. But R-parity assures that the decay of a superpartner has to include a lighter superpartner among its decay products, so all of the superpartners that remained after annihilation stopped eventually decayed into the lightest one, which is still around. The lightest superpartner is some admixture of the fermionic partners of the photon, the Z and the electrically neutral Higgs particles. Whether or not one gets the observed amount of dark matter depends on the masses of the supersymmetric partners and how they mix with one another to form the lightest, stable superpartner. In addition to the search for superpartners at the LHC, there is a lot of activity in trying to directly detect the dark matter that surrounds us.

Cosmological observation has made tremendous advances in pinning down the composition of the universe. It gets less than 5% of its energy density (energy per unit volume) from ordinary matter and about 25% from dark matter. The rest of it resides in something even more mysterious, called "dark energy." Measurement of its properties are consistent with the dark energy arising from a constant background energy density that exists everywhere at all times. This could arise from the non-vanishing value of a scalar field. However the observed energy density would correspond to a field value of a few hundredths of an electron volt (curiously, about the same value as the measured neutrino mass differences), as compared with, for example, the Higgs field value of about 250 billion electron volts. So the mystery is not why there is dark energy, but why there is not a whole lot more. For a long time it was believed that there was zero dark energy, and that some day we might find a symmetry to explain why. For example there is no dark energy, or "cosmological constant," in a theory with unbroken supersymmetry — but that's not the world we live in. We know that the Higgs field exists, and our attempts to understand physics beyond

Teaching at UCB circa 1982. From the Emilio Segré Archives.

the Standard Model predict that other, much stronger fields should also exist. We have as yet no understanding (other than anthropic) as to how the energy in all these fields gets canceled, leaving only a tiny sliver, that nevertheless forms the major part of the energy density in the universe today.

The development and confirmation of the Standard Model was a remarkable achievement of modern particle physics, culminating in the announcement on July 4, 2012, of the discovery of the Higgs boson. But there remain many fascinating unanswered questions. Whether the means to fully address these questions will be provided by the world community is itself an unanswered question.

Reflections

I became a feminist by necessity. My passion was physics. My feminism was a byproduct of the obstacles that I faced in that pursuit. I remember that a remark I made to my friend Grace Spruch after reading the autobiography of Fay Ajzenberg-Selove (*A Matter of Choices: Memoirs of a Female Physicist*, Rutgers University Press, 1994) elicited the response from Grace: "I guess you're more of a physicist than a feminist." This has probably been reflected in my attitudes towards physics throughout my career, and particularly in my positions on committees such as the very difficult 1983 HEPAP Subpanel, or the nearly as difficult 1992 Subpanel. I had no appetite for political jockeying; I was interested only in the best physics results. In 1983 there had been perhaps some part of me that wanted the US to "beat" CERN, because of my poor treatment there. I lost, and the country lost, on that account. Preeminence in high energy physics, which was once the providence of the United States, has been essentially given up to Europe and Japan. So we had to learn to adapt. But as my National Science Board colleague, the mathematician Richard Tapia, liked to tell me, I "think like a physicist," meaning, I guess, that I instinctively use logical reasoning, as opposed to emotional responses or politically motivated rationales in decision making.

I also have little patience for the notion, fashionable in some feminist circles, that science dominated by women would be different from science dominated by men. I can imagine, as my colleague Gordy Kane once remarked, that in some fields, for example, applied science, medical science or anthropology, women might naturally be drawn to particular areas of study that men are less apt to consider investigating. But science is science. Its predictions and conjectures are testable: verifiable or refutable by direct observation and/or by the logic of mathematics. Maybe women would have given different names to what we observe, but the observations and the inferences about nature would be the same.

Not surprisingly, I was disturbed by the sociologist Andrew Pickering's view of the science in which I had participated, as expressed in his book *Constructing Quarks: A Sociological History of Particle Physics* (University Press, Edinburgh, UK, 1984). He describes scientific findings not as the results of experimental observation, but rather as a construct emerging from the sociology of interactions among experimentalists and theorists. In short profiles of John Ellis, Alvaro De Rujula and myself, he focuses on the specific struggle among the advocates of charm and those of colored states as the interpretation of the new physics, that John and I had debated with John Ward in the immediate aftermath of the November Revolution of 1974. Pickering's discussion implies that the conclusion in favor of charm was not the result of what the data told us, but rather the result of a consensus reached by the particle physics community, much in the same way that a consensus is reached for a political candidate or the winner of a beauty contest. It was somewhat unsettling to find myself described as an "opportunist": my two colleagues and I were schooled in the "old physics," but switched to the "new physics" when the opportunity arose.

It is true that experiments often get it wrong (as more often than not do theorists) on a first attempt to measure (or to interpret) a new phenomenon. (The results emerging from the LHC have been remarkably free of such hiccups so far.) For as long as I can remember, just about every first measurement in weak interactions initially had results that turned out to be incorrect, starting from the structure of the Fermi couplings in nuclear beta-decay through the false "discovery" of supersymmetry at the CERN SPS when it first started operations. Included in this list are two incorrect results that I spent some time on myself, the decay of a kaon into a pion and two leptons, discussed in some detail earlier — with the same incorrect result found in two different experiments — and the decay of a kaon into two muons, which a 1971 experiment at LBL had failed to detect, setting (erroneously) a limit below the minimal decay rate predicted by very basic concepts like the conservation of probability. In many cases the reason for the initial incorrect result was never pinned down. However, it is hardly the case that one (or the community) simply stops when some experiment finds the desired or expected answer. A result is not accepted by the community as conclusive until it has been independently corroborated by others. More importantly, one day's new physics becomes the next day's background and/or the standard for calibration in searches for yet newer physics. This requires a level of certainty that would not be possible if the earlier results were not thoroughly studied and understood in detail. Most often, new pictures of nature do not invalidate older ones, although it takes some physicists longer than others to accept the new. Neither quantum mechanics nor relativity invalidated Newtonian mechanics, which remains the correct description of nature over sufficiently large distances, with sufficiently small energies and velocities, where the effects of quantum mechanics and of Einstein's relativity can be neglected. Nor did the Standard Model invalidate Fermi theory as the correct low energy description of weak interactions, or the low energy description of strong interactions in terms of hadrons rather than quarks. If a 10-dimensional string theory, or an 11-dimensional M-theory, is one day shown to underlie the field theories of the four forces of nature, the latter will continue to correctly describe the physics observed in present day laboratory experiments and in cosmological observations.

* * *

I was the first woman faculty member in the Berkeley physics department, consisting at the time of nearly 60 active faculty, almost all full professors. I was also the sole woman member of numerous national committees for many years. I was so accustomed to this that it took me by surprise when my parents joined me at the close of the 1992 HEPAP Subpanel meeting at Hilton Head, an island resort town off the South Carolina coast, and, after poking his head into the meeting, my father exclaimed in awe: "You're the only woman!" When I was elected to the National Academy of Sciences in 1991, the only other women in the Physics Section were C. S. Wu and Trudi Goldhaber, elected in 1958 and 1972, the second and third women physicists elected to the Academy. The first was Nobelist Maria Goeppert Mayer, elected in 1956. (The anatomist Florence Rena Sabin was the first woman member of the NAS, elected in 1925.) The astrophysicist Margaret Geller joined us in 1992, but after the deaths of

Wu in 1997 and Goldhaber in 1998 we remained at two women until my fellow particle theorist Helen Quinn was elected in 2003.

Now there are seven women among 55 active[27] physics faculty at Berkeley, or 11% of active faculty; these are all very self-confident and successful women. A number of younger women, including alumnae of the 1981 Les Houches summer school, have emerged to fill the ranks of the various committees I once served on. (I was however taken aback when as late as 2007 I found myself once again the only woman on the rather large technical review committee for a national lab. A refreshing counter-experience was the National Science Board with 24 members, almost all Clinton appointees, and 25–30% women in various STEM fields throughout my six-year tenure.) By April 2013 the female contingent of the NAS Physics Section stood at 10 out of about 200.

There has also been a profound change in attitudes among men. When I was a student at Case and at Brookhaven/Columbia, more than one of my fellow students explained that he wanted to marry a smart, educated woman so that she would be his intellectual equal, but he would expect her not to work. (I found this pretty appalling.) Now nearly all of my younger male colleagues have professional wives, and fully respect professional women, including those in their own field. Even men of an older generation have changed their views after their daughters grew up in an era when women had more expectations and opportunities. Some have come to me for advice on how to encourage daughters who are aspiring physicists. One man who asked me to write a letter to his daughter probably didn't remember the disparaging remarks about women in physics he had made to me on a visit to CERN when I was a young student there.

Why, then, is it still true that many of our women graduate students are less self-confident and self-assertive than their male counterparts? I'm not making this up. There have been American Physical Society (APS) visits to our department — as well as other review committees — that prompted conversations with women graduate students. The faculty members involved — male and female, myself included — were shocked

---

[27] Meaning still teaching, unlike myself; I am one of about 40 living emeriti, the others all male.

to learn that women graduate students still experience disparaging, and even sexually offensive, remarks from their male peers. And we heard the age-old complaint that men are very sure of themselves, even when they don't know what they are talking about — and that women are still reluctant to speak up in class or in group meetings.

There seem to be very subtle cultural influences that I don't understand, and I have no idea how they can be controlled. For example, my first two children, a boy and a girl, just a year apart in age, played with all the same toys at home. We had no television, and only farmers as neighbors. Yet one day when Alain was two or three, I took him to CERN; as we were leaving the car, he pulled out the doll that he had brought along with him, but then suddenly turned back, saying: "I can't take this doll with me." Where did he learn that boys were not supposed to play with dolls? When we visited Dominique's high school in Switzerland, her physics teacher told us that she had excelled until the boys in the class started making fun of her because she readily answered questions. My heart sank. Why was this still happening? (It hadn't even happened to me.) Perhaps because she was then in a private school with young boys from very privileged families, who thought they owned the world? Is there still an element of this in what we are hearing from women graduate students today? Old habits, old realities and stereotypes die hard and influence us all. Once at the Heathrow airport, it took about a half an hour for my woman chauffeur from Rutherford Laboratory and I to find each other, because we were both looking for a man. As a very small child, I insisted on referring to our female doctor as "Nurse Pierce," because despite what my parents told me, I could not believe that a woman was a doctor.

There was a brilliant, energetic and enthusiastic young woman physicist with whom I worked on the CSWP. A year after she left the committee, she committed suicide in her home when her husband and children were away. Was she overwhelmed by the pressure of keeping up an apparently successful career while caring for a family? The surprise and shock we felt at this news prompted the comment from another CSWP committee member that maybe we were misguided in telling women that they can "have it all." I prefer to think not, but that was a very disturbing event for those of us involved in promoting women in physics.

Another disturbing experience for me came with the Clarence Thomas/ Anita Hill hearings which took place after Thomas had been nominated to the Supreme Court and Hill accused him of sexual harassment when she was under his supervision as a young lawyer. I found myself unable to turn off the TV during the hearings, pacing the floor while being flooded with suppressed memories. Among the generally clueless reactions of the all-male Senate Judiciary Committee members, the most offensive to me was the inference that Hill should have resigned if she was uncomfortable with Thomas' advances. The idea that a woman should abandon her career aspirations because of the inappropriate behavior of a male superior was unacceptable. I also identified with the woman lawyer who testified that she still exchanged Christmas cards with people who had made inappropriate advances. That's just the way things were for any woman in a male-dominated profession when there was no such thing as affirmative action or consciousness raising. The difference in the Thomas case was that his very positions — Assistant Secretary of Education for the Office for Civil Rights and Chairman of the Equal Employment Opportunity Commission — should have precluded such behavior.

I was not the only one affected by the hearings. The day the Judiciary Committee was to vote, I went to LBL and found our administrative assistants, Betty Moura and Luanne Neumann, barricading my office like a two-person army or police force. We were on very good terms, largely because when I had become group leader, I was able to dispel an atmosphere of mistrust that had developed between the scientific and administrative staff — perhaps because I more naturally viewed the latter as people rather than as servants. In addition I tried very hard to get Luanne reclassified to a higher salary category. At some point I came armed with a list of DOE recommendations that a group of 10 or 20 women, including myself, had been asked to come up with.[28] The list explicitly recommended reclassification. Although I had the support of Bob Birge, former Physics Division Director and at the time its Deputy

---

[28] One of my recommendations was to avoid appointing women to too many committees. Sweden had passed a law requiring every committee to include a woman member. My old friend Celelia Jarlskog, at the time the sole woman physicist in the country, bore the brunt of that well-intentioned attempt to promote gender diversity.

Director, I did not succeed. Now Betty and Luanne wanted me to send a letter to Joe Biden, the Senate Judiciary Committee chair. I had recently been elected to the National Academy of Sciences, and they thought my letter might have some clout. They faxed the letter the same day, but I think it didn't get through before the vote. (I did get a nice answer from Senator Biden.)

* * *

It has often been asserted by women in physics that their prospects were better in Europe, at least in France and in Southern Europe, than in the US. In my experience, that was because more women *entered* the field (perhaps because there was no one who told them that it was a "singularly unfeminine profession"), but it was also the case that the glass ceiling was very low for women, much lower than in the US by the time I returned. It is true that I gravitated to the highest rank in the CNRS, and that there were examples of highly respected women in French and Italian physics (no less than twice Nobelist Marie Curie), but these were very rare. A French friend of my son Bruno who was visiting the Bay Area, and whose mother was a physicist, told me (a bit to my embarrassment) how much his mother talked about me as "*La femme qui est respect´ee commme les hommes*" (the women who is as respected as the men) — in other words, an exception to the rule. Europe (especially Germany) has changed a lot in this regard since I left, but during my time there, it seemed that in Europe there were fewer barriers to entering our field for a woman, but more to advancing in it. I think that the latter had to do with a still hierarchical society in Europe and a more pragmatic one in the US, at least at the time of my return in 1981. If a woman was recognized as the person to get the job done she would be the one hired. My friend Jacques Prentki once remarked that all the successful women physicists were trained in Europe. That had a lot of truth to it, but many of them got good jobs in the US. In my own case, it was undoubtedly helpful that I had a research position during my childbearing years without the pressure of teaching and "getting tenure" in the US university system. However, at some point I had hit a brick wall in the very place where I was producing influential research. And so I left.

The situation in the Warsaw pact countries was much worse, in spite of their "perfectly egalitarian" socialist societies. In the summer of 1980,

I attended a conference in Hungary. Dimitri, who was also supposed to come, cancelled at the last minute, and I was asked to give his talk as well as my own. So I spent a lot of time preparing transparencies. I don't remember exactly what my own talk was about, but I remember that Dimitri's was on the interface of particle physics and cosmology, because a famous Russian cosmologist, Yakov Zel'dovich, was also in attendance, and he knew a lot more cosmology than I did. Fortunately he was not so familiar with the particle physics aspects of it that I spoke about. He was not allowed to travel to the West, presumably because he had worked on the Soviet nuclear program. In the usual Soviet tradition, he invited me for a private conversation, which unfortunately turned out to be a little awkward. He was urging me to make another visit to the Soviet Union, but this was at the time when the physicists Andrei Sakharov, Yuri Orlov and Natan Sharanksy were in exile or imprisoned, and there was an international effort (that had been initiated by Berkeley physicists) to obtain their freedom, by, among other things, a moratorium on scientific cooperation with the Soviet Union. So in spite of my many friends there, I was somewhat ambivalent about visiting at that time, and was unsure how to respond without offending him.

The CERN report on women had been distributed a few months earlier, and I was also asked to lead a discussion session on women in physics. There were a few younger women who participated in the discussion, but many women remained silent throughout. Among the older men standing in the back looking rather like security guards, I am sure that there were some who were present, not because the topic was of interest to them, but to make sure that no one said anything out of line.

* * *

This book has been an account of my professional life as a woman in physics. I have intentionally avoided details of my family life except as it intersected with the professional. I have no wish to air the marital difficulties that led to my divorce and remarriage. However there were some sources of strain that were cultural, rather than personal, and more relevant to the story being told here.

As hard as it might have been for a woman to enter a career in physics in the early 1960s, it was no picnic to be married to one who did. Once my career started to take off, Jean-Marc had to endure comments like: "How does it feel to have a famous wife?" In 1969 I was invited by my old friend Bob Adair to speak at an APS meeting in Cambridge, MA (which included a session on women in physics during which the former CERN Director General Viki Weisskopf remarked to me that I was the only woman invited speaker). The meeting fell during our Christmas ski holiday, so I took a train to Geneva from the village of le Chable, at the

foot of the mountain where we skied, and flew to Boston. I remember the year because I turned 30 in 1969, at the height of civil rights and antiwar protests, when everyone over 30 was supposedly suspect. Like my mother and my daughter I looked younger than my age; I had a long and congenial conversation with a young woman sitting next to me on the plane, who was absolutely flabbergasted when she learned that I was *actually 30*. A few months later, Bob invited Jean-Marc to speak at another APS meeting on his work on strange baryon decays. One of his collaborators (who perhaps thought that he should have been invited instead) asserted that I had arranged for Bob to extend the invitation during my trip to Boston, which was not the case. These are but two examples of the pernicious influence of the culture at that time. There is an interesting book by Elga Wasserman, *The Door in the Dream* (NAS, 2000), based on her interviews with women members of the National Academy of Sciences. She groups the women according to the decade in which they were born. It is telling that among the women in my decade, the 1930s — I was born in 1939 — who came of professional age during the growth of the women's movement, a substantial number were divorced as compared with previous decades. Happily, the couples in subsequent generations have fared much better.

Acronyms

AIP: American Institute of Physics

APS: American Physical Society

ATLAS: A Toroidal LHC Apparatus, one of two large "multipurpose" detectors at the LHC

BEGN: Buras–Ellis–Gaillard–Nanopoulos

BNL: Brookhaven National Laboratory, Upton, Long Island, NY

CBA: Colliding Beam Accelerator, a facility planned to be built at BNL, but discontinued in 1983

CERN: *Organisation Européen pour la Recherche Nucléaire* (European Organization for Nuclear Research), originally *Conseil Européen pour la Recherche Nucléaire*, headquartered in Meyrin (Geneva), Switzerland, and now extending into France under the foothills of the Jura mountains

CMS: Compact Muon Solenoid, one of two large "multipurpose" detectors at the LHC

CNRS: *Centre National de la Recherche Scientifique* (National Center for Scientific Research), France

CSWP: Committee on the Status of Women in Physics of the APS

DESY: *Deutsches Elektronen-Synchrotron* (German Electron Synchrotron), Hamburg, Germany

DOE: Department of Energy

EGMZ: Ellis–Gaillard–Maiani–Zumino

GHMR: Gross–Harvey–Martinec–Rohm

GIM: Glashow–Iliopoulos–Maiani. The "GIM mechanism" refers to the cancellation of higher order weak interaction contributions among quarks of different flavors.

GLR: Gaillard–Lee–Rosner

GQW: Georgi–Quinn–Weinberg

GUT: Grand Unified Theory, referring to the class of theories that embeds the three gauge theories of the Standard Model into a single gauge theory

GWS: Glashow–Weinberg–Salam, the theorists credited with the elucidation of the electroweak theory of the Standard Model

HEPAP: High Energy Physics Advisory Panel to the DOE (subsequently also to the NSF)

ICFA: International Committee for Future Accelerators

ICHEP: International Conference on High Energy Physics

ITEP: Institute for Theoretical and Experimental Physics, Moscow, Russia

IHEP: Institute for High Energy Physics, Serpukov, Russia

LAPP: *Laboratoire d'Annecy-le-Vieux de Physique des Particules* (Annecy-le-Vieux Laboratory for Particle Physics), Annecy-le-Vieux, France

LBL: Lawrence Berkeley Laboratory, Berkeley, CA. Later renamed Lawrence Berkeley National Laboratory (LBNL)

LEP: Large Electron–Positron Collider, at CERN

LHC: Large Hadron Collider, at CERN

NAS: National Academy of Sciences

NSB: National Science Board

NSF: National Science Foundation

PEP: Positron–Electron Project, at SLAC

PRD: *Physical Review D*, the particle physics section of the APS journal *Physical Review*

QCD: Quantum chromodynamics, the theory of strong interactions in the Standard Model

QED: Quantum electrodynamics, the theory of electric and magnetic interactions

RHIC: Relativistic Heavy Ion Collider, Brookhaven, Long Island

SCNC: Strangeness changing neutral currents

SLAC: Stanford Linear Accelerator Center, Menlo Park, CA
SPEAR: Stanford Positron Electron Asymmetric Rings, at SLAC
SPS: Super Proton Synchrotron, the CERN proton–antiproton collider
SSC: Superconducting Super Collider, the proton–proton collider that was to have been built in Waxahachie, TX, but was canceled in 1993
STEM: Science, Technology, Engineering and Math
SVZ: Shifman–Vainshtein–Zakharov
UC: University of California
UCB: University of California at Berkeley
URA: Universities Research Association, a consortium of universities that oversees Fermilab
UW: University of Washington, Seattle, WA

Glossary

Abelian: See boxes on pages 57 and 58.

Accelerator: A facility, usually a circular ring, in which particles are speeded up (accelerated) by electric fields with their trajectory bent, for example into a circle, by surrounding magnetic fields.

Asymptotic freedom: The property of a theory in which the force among particles becomes weaker as their total energy increases (or when the distance separating them decreases).

Baryon: See Hadron.

Boson: A particle with integer spin in units of Planck's constant $\hbar$.

Bound state: A composite state made of more elementary constituents. Examples are 1) the atom, composed of electrons and nuclei, 2) the nucleus, composed of protons and neutrons, 3) the proton, composed of two up quarks and a down quark.

Charge conjugation (C): An operation that turns a particle into its antiparticle.

Charged current: This expression refers to processes involving both quarks (or hadrons) and leptons, in which both the quark and lepton electric charges change by one unit.

Charmonium: A bound state composed of a charm quark and its antiparticle.

Chiral symmetry: Symmetry under a group of transformations that act differently on right-spinning and left-spinning quarks.

Collider: A facility, usually circular, with two beams of particles traveling in opposite directions, that interact at various points along their trajectories. Colliders have the advantage that all of the energy in the beams can be converted into mass: $E = mc^2$.

Color: See Flavor.

Complex number: A complex number can be written as $a + ib$, or as $\rho e^{i\phi}$, where a, b, ρ and ϕ are real numbers, and i is an imaginary number of unit length defined by $i^2 = -1$. The magnitude, or absolute value, of the complex number is given by $\sqrt{a^2 + b^2}$ or, equivalently, by ρ. A complex number of unit magnitude can be written in the form $e^{i\phi}$. As ϕ varies from 0 to 2π, this complex number traces out a circle of unit length centered at the origin of the complex plane, where the x-axis, or horizontal axis (abscissa), represents real numbers, and the y-axis, or vertical axis (ordinate), represents imaginary numbers. In QED, for example, a symmetry operation is multiplication by $e^{i\phi_p}$ on each particle p, with ϕ_p proportional to the electric charge Q_p of the particle.

Coupling constant: A number whose square determines the probability for an interaction (or "coupling") to occur. In quantum theory this number is not really a "constant," but depends on the energy exchanged among the particles in the interaction.

CP: The combined charge conjugation (C) and parity (P) operations.

Decay: The process by which a particle disappears, leaving a collection of lighter particles (the decay products) in its place.

Electron volt: The amount of energy acquired by an electron traversing an electric potential of one volt.

Electroweak: Referring to the theory that incorporates both the weak and electromagnetic interactions in the Standard Model, also known as the GWS theory.

Fermion: A particle with half-integer spin in units of Planck's constant $\hbar$; no two fermions can occupy the same state.

Flavor: A quantum number, such as electric charge, isospin, strangeness or charm, that distinguishes different quarks and different leptons from one another. Flavor is distinct from "color" the "chromodynamic charge" of QCD. Every quark of a given flavor has three possible colors.

Gauge symmetry: A symmetry under a group of transformations that act differently at different points in space and time. See pages 57 and 58.

GeV: Giga (billion) electron volts.

Hadron: A strongly interacting particle. This term was introduced by Lev Okun in 1962 from the Greek word "*hadros,*" which he defined as "heavy" or "massive" (the known hadrons were heavier than the known leptons). The English Wiktionary defines it as "thick," and the French one as "*fort*" which indeed means "strong." Hadrons with half-integer spin are called baryons, and those with integer spin are called mesons. The earliest known baryons (proton, neutron, Λ, ...) were heavier than the known mesons (π, K, ...), which in turn were heavier than the known leptons (e, μ, ν). This accounts for the names from the Greek words "*barys*" (heavy), "*mesos*" (middle) and "*leptos*" (light).

Hiesenberg's uncertainty principle: The statement that time (t) and energy (E), or position (r) and momentum (p), cannot be known with absolute precision; the uncertainty (Δ) in these quantities is determined by Planck's constant: $\Delta t \Delta E = \Delta r \Delta p = \hbar$. For a particle of mass m moving with a velocity v much smaller than the speed of light c (thirty trillion centimeters per second) $p = mv$; for a particle with v very close to c, $p = E/c$. (See also Planck's constant.)

Isospin: The group of rotations in an abstract space that can turn an up quark into a down quark and therefore, for example, a proton into a neutron. See page 39. This is sometime called isotopic spin by particle physicists, which is really a misnomer because isotopes, which have the same number of protons (the same "atomic number" or electric charge) but different numbers of neutrons (and therefore different atomic weights), are not related by isospin. Nuclear physicists more correctly use the term isobaric spin; isobars, with the same number of nucleons (atomic weight) but different numbers of protons, are directly related by isospin transformations.

Left-spinning: With spin oriented opposite to the direction of motion, like a left-handed screw.

Lepton: A fermion with no strong interactions, including the three negatively charged leptons e, μ, τ, their associated neutrinos, and the antiparticles of these. (See also Hadron.)

Meson: See Hadron.

Neutral current: This expression refers to processes involving both quarks (or hadrons) and leptons, in which the quark and lepton electric charges remain unchanged.

Nucleon: A proton or a neutron.

Parity (P): The operation that changes the directions of motion of particles. If the particles are lying in a plane, P is equivalent to mirror reflection in that plane.

Parton: An elementary constituent of a proton or a neutron, a term coined by Richard Feynman. In the Standard Model the partons include quarks, antiquarks and gluons.

Pauli exclusion principle: The statement that two fermions cannot occupy the same state.

Planck energy: About a trillion trillion trillion times the proton mass of a billion electron volts, the energy at which gravitational effects become strong.

Planck length: About a billionth of a trillionth of a trillionth of a centimeter, the distance within which gravitational effects become strong.

Planck's constant: Denoted by $\hbar$, it characterizes the (small) distances and (high) energies where quantum effects become important. It is equal to a ten thousandth of a trillionth of an electron volt times a second, or in units where the velocity (speed) of light is one, twenty trillionths of an electron volt times a centimeter.

Quantum numbers: The values of the various attributes of a particle. These include spin, as well as *intrinsic* quantum numbers: flavor and color.

Resonance: In the context used in this book, a resonance is a bound state of quarks that is heavy enough to decay rapidly via strong interactions into lighter quark bound states.

Right-spinning: With spin oriented in the direction of motion, like a right-handed screw.

Scalar: An entity that is invariant under rotations in space. It has no direction, only magnitude. A scalar *boson* has no spin and is the particle associated with a scalar *field* with only one spatial component.

Spin: The rotational motion of a particle, similar to that of a spinning top. Particle spins are always integer multiples of $\frac{1}{2}\hbar$, where $\hbar$ is Planck's constant.

Spontaneous symmetry breaking: A situation in which the world we observe does not respect the symmetry of the laws of physics. See page 80.

Supersymmetry: A symmetry among fermions and bosons. See pages 107–109.

TeV: Tera (trillion) electron volts.

Vector: An entity that has spatial direction as well as magnitude. A vector *boson* has one unit of spin, and is the particle associated with a vector *field* with more than one spatial component; the number of components depends on the dimension of space and whether or not the particle is massive.

Wavelength: The length of a single oscillation in a wave. For example X-rays, blue light, red light, and radio waves are electromagnetic waves, listed in order of increasing wavelength. Any particle can be described in terms of a wave whose wavelength decreases as its energy increases.